Family Foster Care in the Next Century

Family Foster Care in the Next Century

Kathy Barbell and Lois Wright, editors

Transaction Publishers
New Brunswick (U.S.A.) and London (U.K.)

This book is printed on acid-free paper that meets the American National Standard
for Permanence of Paper for Printed Library Materials.

Library of Congress Catalog Number: 00–027302
ISBN: 0–7658–0712–2
Printed in the United States of America

Library of Congress Cataloging-in-Publication Data

Family foster care in the next century / Kathy Barbell and Lois Wright, editors.
    p. cm.
    Includes bibliographical references.
    ISBN 0-7658-0712-2 (pbk. : alk. paper)
    1. Foster home care—United States.   2. Family social work—United
States.   I. Barbell, Kathy.   II. Wright, Lois, 1942–.
    HV863 .F37   2000
    362.73'3'0973—dc21   00-027302
                                                   CIP

501-14
138876

CONTENTS

PROMOTING CHILD WELL-BEING

Family Foster Care in the Next Century

Although family foster care, designed to provide temporary protection and nurturing for children experiencing maltreatment, has been a critical service for millions of children in the United States, the increased attention given to this service in the last two decades has focused more on its limited ability to achieve its intended outcomes than on its successes. This has resulted in a questioning and devaluing of family foster care as well as predictions of drastic reductions in its use. The reality, however, has been quite different. Though the use of the service has shifted, reflecting social and political events, family foster care remains an important child welfare service.

Reaffirming its commitment to family foster care, the Child Welfare League of America's National Advisory Committee on Family Foster Care recommended that a special issue of *Child Welfare* be published on the subject. Aware that recent history has shown out-of-home care reacting to rather than anticipating change, the Committee decided to focus the special issue on family foster care in the next century. This issue would thus provide the opportunity for the field's best practitioners, researchers, and managers to share their knowledge as well as their expectations, concerns, and hopes for family foster care.

Acting on the Committee's recommendation, a call for abstracts was issued in the fall of 1997, with overwhelming results: three times the number of abstracts usually submitted for a special issue were received. Both the range of content addressed and the quality of the abstracts received were impressive, making selection of the 11 articles included in this issue difficult. The need to consider balance and coverage of specific topics necessitated the exclusion of many fine papers.

1

Immediately after CWLA issued the call for abstracts, Congress enacted major federal legislation impacting family foster care—the Adoption and Safe Families Act of 1997 (P.L. 105–89)—reminding us of the importance of legislation as it reflects social trends and political thinking and shapes practice. A review of that act, as well as other major child welfare legislation, provides an important contextual element for this volume.

In 1980, in response to the "drifting" of children in care, Congress passed the Adoption Assistance and Child Welfare Act of 1980 (P.L. 96-272), a key factor in shaping the current status of family foster care. The legislation responded to concerns that placement in out-of-home care was being used when other services were more appropriate, that children were remaining in care for excessive periods of time, and that children were simply being forgotten once they entered out-of-home care. The goal of the act was to reduce reliance on out-of-home care and encourage the use of preventive and reunification services; it also mandated that agencies engage in permanency planning efforts.

By 1984, P.L. 96-272 was showing some success in reducing the number of children in care and the length of time spent in care. From the mid-1980s to the late 1990s, however, a dramatic 74% increase in the number of children in out-of-home care occurred [Petit & Curtis 1997]; the length of time children remained in care and their rate of reentry into care also rose. Concurrently, the out-of-home care system found itself facing new challenges: the overrepresentation of children of color; an influx of infants and preschoolers; children with increasingly severe emotional/behavioral problems; the pervasiveness of substance abuse and its impact on families; the growing number of children infected/affected by HIV/AIDS; and the discharge of many youths from care who lacked jobs, homes, and connections to a family.*

---

* In 1986 Congress amended the federal foster care program to create the Independent Living Services program, a relatively small program designed to provide services and supports to enhance independent living skills of youths who had not been reunified or adopted and who would remain in care until they "aged out."

Once again, the out-of-home care system found itself straining to deal with the sheer number of children in the system and with the complex issues that had brought them there. Concern grew that many children were coming into care needlessly and that many more could go home or achieve permanency with another family if more family-centered, intensive services were available. Congress again took action, creating the Family Preservation and Family Support program as part of the Omnibus Budget Reconciliation Act of 1993. This program reiterated the principles of P.L. 96-272 but added funding for a variety of services, including intensive family preservation services (intended to keep families together) and services to reunify families with children in care.

Despite the mandates and funding of the Family Preservation and Family Support program, the child welfare system continued to struggle to provide the level of services needed for children to achieve timely permanence, the number of children in out-of-home care continued to increase in most states, and a significant percentage of children experienced increased stays in care. Large caseloads, inexperienced and untrained staff, and high turnover rates of workers and foster parents made it difficult for children and families to obtain the help they needed. In response, in late 1997, Congress passed the Adoption and Safe Families Act (ASFA); President Clinton signed it into law on November 17, 1997. The new legislation reauthorized the Family Preservation and Family Support program, renamed it the Promoting Safe and Stable Families program, and modified and clarified a wide range of policies established under the Adoption Assistance and Child Welfare Act of 1980, including:

- modifying the "reasonable efforts" states must make to preserve or reunite families by providing examples of circumstances in which states are not required to make efforts to keep children with their parents for safety reasons.
- establishing (for the first time in federal law) timelines and conditions for filing termination of parental rights petitions.

States must file on behalf of any child, regardless of age, who has been in care for 15 of the most recent 22 months.
- setting new timeframes for permanency hearings at 12 months rather than 18 months. At a permanency hearing, there must be a determination of whether and when a child will be returned home, placed for adoption, or referred for legal guardianship or another planned permanent living arrangement.
- encouraging adoptions by requiring states to make reasonable efforts and to document child-specific efforts to place a child for adoption, and by providing "bonuses" for the adoption of children with special needs previously in care.
- continuing and expanding the Promoting Safe and Stable Families program to include funding for time-limited reunification and adoption promotion and support services.

To comply with the law, public and private agencies must initiate significant program and practice changes in the coming years. The articles in this special issue provide guidance on improving permanency outcomes and child well-being, the cornerstones of ASFA.

Responding to the Need for Change

As social and political trends and new legislation evolve to reshape child welfare, policymakers and service providers continue to offer innovative policy and practice options, as demonstrated through the number and variety of submissions received in response to *Child Welfare*'s call for abstracts. Areas of concern included the following:

- *Meeting the needs of special populations.* Abstracts addressed children who are seriously emotionally disturbed (SED), medically fragile infants, infants and toddlers entering care, adolescents aging out of care, and youths who are lesbian, gay, transgender, bisexual, or presenting other sexual identity issues.

- *Recruiting and retaining high-quality family foster caregivers.* Abstracts addressed strategies for recruitment that involve various sectors of the community; determining exceptional versus abusive homes; specialized training to increase the competence of parents fostering prenatally substance exposed infants; planned and emergency respite care; using foster caregivers as resources for children and their families, particularly in relation to treatment for SED; professional, salaried inner-city foster parents; and a redefinition of foster parents as extended family who continue to have involvement with children after reunification.
- *Kinship care.* Abstracts addressed both informal and formal kinship care; regulatory procedures—monitoring, compliance, and ongoing risk assessment—and their effect on family life; the dual role as family member and foster parent; and supports for kinship parents. Recognizing the importance of kinship care, CWLA published a special issue of *Child Welfare* on the subject in September 1996.
- *Mandates for expedited permanency.* Abstracts addressed the expanding infant and preschooler population in care; arrangements for early assessment and intervention by interdisciplinary teams; public-private collaboration to provide mandated health/mental health screening; and concurrent planning, especially for substance-affected infants or other children at high risk of foster care drift. To expedite reunification, abstracts discussed increased services to biological families; providing for child safety while rehabilitating parents; arranging biological family contact according to such factors as the child's emotional readiness and developmental stage; and providing immediate foster care placement rather than temporary shelter.
- *Family supportive, community-based care.* Both current philosophy and new legislation are impelling us toward identifying new models of intervention that respect, preserve, and strengthen family-child ties and that reflect the sig-

nificance and power of communities as resources to families. Abstracts described programs for transitional housing for homeless women and their children; parenting apprenticeships; shared family care; placing foster children within their home neighborhoods and using foster parents as resources for biological parents; and therapeutic communities.

- *Service delivery and funding arrangements.* Abstracts dealt with collaboration in service delivery, particularly in relation to community-based services for SED children and early intervention for infants and preschoolers; the use of contractual services; managed care, particularly in relation to meeting the health and mental health needs of SED and medically fragile children; increasing flexibility and finding alternatives to rigidly defined service boundaries and categorical funding; and increased funding.

- *Cultural issues.* As the cultural mosaic of America is changing, so must the cultural sensitivity and responsiveness of child welfare services. Abstracts focused on African American children and youths and the service implications of culture-related responses to abuse; the need for and obstacles to recruiting Asian foster parents; and American Indian family issues.

- *Outcomes and accountability.* Outcomes and accountability were subthemes in most of the abstracts submitted, and the call for more sophisticated and informative evaluation and appropriate measures recurred. One difficult and provocative issue raised was defining and documenting accountability when responsibility for services is broadly dispersed throughout a community. Other abstracts reviewed measures of child well-being, reported on the use of children's voices in program evaluation, and provided a variety of perspectives on using data to understand and improve policy and services.

Preview of Articles Selected for Inclusion

To give adequate attention to all the important issues facing family foster care would have required several volumes. The central theme of the articles included in this issue is outcomes accountability, certainly a current driving force in child welfare as well as in other public and private services fields. With new data systems, new funding arrangements, and new calls for evidence that interventions are effective, the importance of outcome accountability can be expected to increase in the next century. The articles are organized into three categories—using data for planning, enhancing outcomes through new models, and promoting child well-being.

Using Data for Planning in Family Foster Care

The Administration on Children, Youth, and Families' Program Instruction [ACYF 1998] regarding the Adoption and Safe Families Act of 1997 (ASFA) underscores the legislation's intent regarding results and addresses the appropriate use of statewide data for planning. Marie Jamieson and Jami M. Bodonyi, in "Data-Driven Child Welfare Policy and Practice in the Next Century," describe how Washington State's Families for Kids used two data systems—the Washington State Children's Administration Case and Management Information System and the Washington State Social Service Payment System—to identify children legally free for adoption and to track their movement through out-of-home care. In so doing, they identified gaps in the information available through these systems and discovered obstacles to permanence. The authors described how data were interpreted and findings carried back to the field to provide a framework for problem solving and continuous improvement of practice to enhance permanency planning.

In "Measuring Performance in Child Welfare: Secondary Effects of Success," Charles L. Usher, Judith B. Wildfire, and Deborah

A. Gibbs report selected results from evaluations of two reform initiatives—Family to Family and Families for Kids—in three states (Alabama, North Carolina, and Ohio) and offer lessons for the development of outcome measurement. Although the evaluations produced positive findings in terms of the children's movement through the out-of-home care system, these successes also had secondary effects, including changes in the population of children entering care and increased staff awareness and understanding of trends in and the need to monitor and use data to shape service responses.

Leslie Wilson and James Conroy's article, "Satisfaction of Children in Out-of-Home Care," serves as a reminder that no system of accountability is complete without the voice of the customer—in this case, the children who have experienced the out-of-home care system. The authors report on four years' data collected through interviews in which children discuss their satisfaction with both their physical environments during placement and their foster families. Results supported the children's ability to assess their own needs and to provide valid information that can be used to improve the out-of-home care system.

Enhancing Outcomes Through New Models of Family Foster Care

Demographic data provide a picture of the population of children who will need family foster care in the next century. Linda Katz, in "Concurrent Planning: Benefits and Pitfalls," describes a model that promotes timely permanence for one significant subgroup of this population—young, chronically neglected children. Katz's article explains the model's history and theoretical underpinnings, target population, core components, common concerns about and pitfalls in implementation, possible outcomes, and evaluation results. The author suggests that the model be viewed as only one approach to enhancing outcomes for some children in care and cautions us not to see concurrent planning, as she has defined it, as the sole and best way to improve outcomes.

Although family foster care provides for the safety of children, the children still experience the emotional and psychological distress caused by the separation from their families. In "Shared Family Care: Providing Services to Parents and Children Placed Together in Out-of-Home Care," Richard P. Barth and Amy Price suggest that a shared family care model can not only eliminate separation trauma but may also expedite permanence and decrease the recurrence of child abuse and neglect and additional placements. They present key elements of the emerging model of shared family care, describe several programs, and discuss how, despite the relatively high cost of shared family care, outcomes (shorter and fewer placements) can result in fiscal savings. Financing such programs and evaluating the results are also addressed.

The proliferation of specialized family foster care programs to meet the needs of children with developmental, behavioral, emotional, or medical needs will most likely continue in the next century. Do these programs provide stable, family-focused, community-based care and achieve permanence for children? In "Professional Foster Care: A Future Worth Pursuing?," Mark F. Testa and Nancy Rolock report on their study of outcomes achieved by professional and specialized family foster care program models in Illinois. Using five criteria, the authors compare the specialized programs' results with the results from the agency's kinship care and nonrelative foster care programs. The findings have implications for child welfare administrators' allocation of limited resources among kinship care, nonrelative foster care, and specialized family foster care programs.

Promoting Child Well-Being in Family Foster Care

The Adoption and Safe Families Act of 1997 "establishes unequivocally that the national goals for children in the child welfare system are safety, permanency, and well-being" [ACYF 1998: 2]. Thus, as states continue to struggle with improving the traditional outcomes of safety and permanency, they must also begin to address the less familiar outcome of child well-being. Currently, clear definitions of child well-being are lacking, as are appropriate, accessible interventions and measures of success.

In "Completing the Evaluation Triangle for the Next Century: Measuring Child 'Well-Being' in Family Foster Care" Sandra J. Altshuler and James P. Gleeson, noting the absence of systematic measures of child well-being in our administrative databases, review the literature regarding how child well-being has been conceptualized and measured. Domains that have been assessed include resilience, coping, and overall functioning; physical health; mental health, including cognitive functioning, developmental delays, behavioral disturbances, and emotional or psychosocial adjustment; and school performance. The authors also discuss the challenge of selecting common measures for incorporation into administrative databases for ongoing monitoring and evaluation.

Considering the large number of very young children now entering family foster care, "Starting Young: Improving the Health and Developmental Outcomes of Infants and Toddlers in the Child Welfare System," describes a collaborative, multidisciplinary, developmental approach to meeting the needs of children in two domains of child well-being—health and developmental needs. Authors Judith Silver, Paul DiLorenzo, Margaret Zukoski, Patricia E. Ross, Barbara J. Amster, and Diane Schlegel discuss the high rates of medical conditions, developmental delays, and mental health problems among children entering care, along with inadequate care related to these conditions. The intervention program on which the authors report is intended to improve health and developmental outcomes of infants in the child welfare system by identifying problems, facilitating access to evaluation and services, establishing interagency linkages and coordination, and training child welfare workers and medical students for better identification of conditions and service provision.

In "Delivering Health and Mental Health Care Services to

Children in Family Foster Care after Welfare and Health Care Reform," Mark D. Simms, Madelyn Freundlich, Ellen S. Battistelli, and Neal D. Kaufman discuss the extensive health and mental health needs of children in family foster care and how reform efforts may impact the health care system's ability to meet those needs. The authors identify major changes brought about by welfare reform, Medicaid managed care, and other health care reforms. Questions are raised about whether reform efforts will address and remove current obstacles to services or add new ones. The connections among children's well-being, access to quality health and mental health care services, and achievement of permanence are discussed, as are the essential features of an effective health care system able to meet the needs of children in care.

Parental drug abuse (particularly maternal use during gestation) is the biggest threat to the well-being of children entering care today and in the next century. Theresa McNichol, in "The Impact of Drug-Exposed Children on Family Foster Care," reports on her study of infants exposed to drugs during gestation and identifies the challenges these young children present and ways the family foster care system can meet them. A series of recommendations is presented on providing quality care; monitoring progress; advocating for and obtaining services for the children and their families; training staff, kinship care providers, foster parents, and biological parents; building relationships with biological families; and assessing intervention effectiveness.

Research by McNichol and others has shown that substance-exposed infants have special caregiving needs. Foster parents, as the primary caregivers, need to know how to meet these needs. In "Evaluation of a Training Program for Foster Parents of Infants with Prenatal Substance Effects," Caroline L. Burry provides information about the effectiveness of a competency-based training program designed to develop the specific skills needed by foster parents to care for infants exposed to drugs prenatally.

Acknowledgments

This special issue would not have been possible without the support of the following individuals, who gave of their time and expertise and served as peer reviewers: *Lou M. Beasley*, Ph.D., Director, Partners in a Planned Community, School of Social Work, Clark Atlanta University, Atlanta, Georgia; *Mark Courtney*, Ph.D., Associate Professor, School of Social Work, University of Wisconsin—Madison; *Anthony Maluccio*, D.S.W., Professor, Graduate School of Social Work, Boston College, Boston, Massachusetts; *Ruth W. Massinga*, Chief Executive Officer, The Casey Family Program, Seattle, Washington; and *Jake Terpstra*, M.S.W., Foster Care Specialist, U.S. Children's Bureau (retired), Grand Rapids, Michigan. Their extensive knowledge and expertise helped us immeasurably as we selected and edited the papers that comprise this issue and its projections for family foster care in the next century.

Kathy Barbell
DIRECTOR OF FOSTER CARE
CHILD WELFARE LEAGUE OF AMERICA
WASHINGTON, DC

Lois Wright
ASSISTANT DEAN
COLLEGE OF SOCIAL WORK
UNIVERSITY OF SOUTH CAROLINA
COLUMBIA, SOUTH CAROLINA

References

Administration on Children, Youth, and Families. (1998). Memo containing program instruction regarding the Adoption and Safe Families Act of 1997. Washington, DC: Author

Petit, M. R., & Curtis, P. A. (1997). *Child abuse and neglect: A look at the states—The 1997 CWLA stat book*. Washington, DC: Child Welfare League of America.

Data-Driven Child Welfare Policy and Practice in the Next Century

1

Marie Jamieson and Jami M. Bodonyi

A great deal of national attention and fiscal incentives are being placed on establishing systems to gather child welfare data. Plentiful data, however, do not guarantee relevant policy development or an impact on practice. This article describes how Washington State Families for Kids used data to create a sense of urgency for system change through distillation and dissemination processes that integrated data, policy, and fieldwork.

Marie Jamieson, M.S.W., is Director, Washington State Families for Kids, Children's Home Society of Washington, Seattle, WA. Jami M. Bodonyi, M.S.W., is Research Associate, Washington State Families for Kids, University of Washington School of Social Work, Northwest Institute for Children and Families, Seattle, WA.

The child welfare field has spent the last few years trying to understand and respond to changes that have occurred since the mid-1980s. The past decade has seen a surge in the number of children in out-of-home care, the number of infants entering care, and the number of children experiencing lengthy stays in care [Goerge et al. 1994; Barth 1997; Spar 1997]. These increases have exacerbated budget strains and prompted calls for accountability: How are public dollars being spent? What is happening to children in the care of the child welfare system?

The development of outcomes in child welfare is being driven by federal accountability rules, the growth of managed care, and class action lawsuits, as well as by a need to understand trends and best practices. State and local data systems have been largely inadequate to address many of the issues raised. Most information systems have focused on funding requirements and gross demographics—hardly tools for management—that are of little or no practical use in the field [Courtney & Collins 1994]. Research, although essential, has usually been so narrow that it is too often viewed as irrelevant or inapplicable to practice by caseworkers. Other times, the amount of data has been so massive that it overwhelms audiences and becomes simpler to ignore than to sift through for meaningful results.

The challenge for child welfare organizations is to gather data relevant to their goals, analyze and distill cogent facts, and relate those facts to practice. To ensure that data are used as motivation to improve practice, dissemination of research findings must overcome the resistance to data that is often prevalent in the field. Several tactics for doing this are discussed in this article: repetition of focused messages, localization of data, mobilization of leadership, and presentation of data within a framework for solutions. To continue providing effective services, practitioners and the administrations that support them must also be able to identify and respond quickly to changing elements in the field. Practice-oriented feedback mechanisms are necessary to track shifts in the field as they occur and to plan for responsive practice. Field workers and managers should be presented with information that has been distilled, but from which they can still draw conclusions and shape their practice. Data should be used to instigate, direct, and monitor change efforts.

This article describes the use of data by Families for Kids (FFK) in Washington State that contributed to the development of new policies and feedback mechanisms within the Department of Social and Health Services (DSHS) and the juvenile court systems.

Families for Kids

FFK is a multiyear, grant-funded initiative to reduce the backlog of children in out-of-home care by reforming the foster care/adoption system in Washington state. Its mission is to ensure timely permanent family connections for all children in state care through reunification with the biological parents, or, when that is not possible, through alternative permanent plans that include adoption and guardianship.*

Authority for FFK to act as a system reform agent arose from the formal partnership and commitment for change secured by a joint grant to DSHS and Children's Home Society of Washington (as the administrative lead of a coalition of private agencies). FFK formed a collaborative coalition of public and private agencies, American Indian tribes, courts, attorneys, court-appointed special advocates, foster parents, and others. FFK staff come from the public and private sectors and work throughout the state to act as a catalyst to the change process.

Defining Areas of Research

FFK began its work for system change by identifying children whose parental rights had been terminated, describing their movement through out-of-home care, and exploring the obstacles

---

* Although permanency is broadly defined, the case studies in this paper are primarily based on children who were adopted.

to their achieving permanence. Permanence for these children most often meant placement with relative or nonrelative families who were able to provide a relationship to the child that would extend into adulthood, through adoption, guardianship, or another alternative. To understand the dynamics contributing to the backlog of children in care, FFK also set out to describe the movement of all Washington state children through out-of-home care, especially those in care longer than one year. Using this information, FFK developed strategies to effect timely permanence from the point of a child's entry into care. Two existing data systems, the Washington State Children's Administration Case and Management Information System (CAMIS), and the Washington State Social Service Payment System (SSPS), which tracks all placements that receive payments from the state, were used as sources.

Two unexpected, yet significant, benefits of the data collection and reporting processes emerged. As FFK began identifying children who were legally free, it soon became apparent that CAMIS did not contain updated information on the legal status of many children. Consequently, FFK staff also used case file reviews and interviews with supervisors and social workers to identify children who were legally free. The asking of basic questions by FFK sparked an awareness of these children and their needs, and planning for many cases was renewed. Additionally, FFK's reporting of findings from the primary case tracking system for the state (CAMIS) back to the field prompted improvements in the timeliness and accuracy of child-level data entered into these systems.

Data as a Change Agent

Unlike many data-based projects, FFK used data as a change agent, rather than solely as an evaluative tool or a mechanism for measurement. Although research is often used to pose questions for examination by the field and to determine foci for reform, FFK used its research findings to inform the development of solutions in the field and to mobilize policy and practice implementation. This approach involved obtaining the investment of everyone from top policymakers to line supervisors and workers in using data as a barometer of performance and as an identifier of problem areas, rather than as a messenger of bad news or as a punitive tool.

Through analysis of the data and interaction with stakeholders at presentations, key points were distilled, enabling all of the players to focus on change efforts that would have the maximum impact. These key points included the following:

1. Infants enter out-of-home care in Washington state in greater numbers than children of other ages: 20% of all children in out-of-home care longer than one year entered care before their first birthdays [English & Clark 1996].

2. Children who are legally free, including infants, experience long lengths of stay. Nearly half of the time spent in care by these children occurs after termination of parental rights (TPR), *even when the child proceeds to adoption or guardianship.* The average length of stay from placement in care to adoption legalization was 45 months; 22 of those months followed TPR [Bodonyi 1997b].

3. A disproportionate number of African American and American Indian children are in care in Washington state: African American children are 4% of the child population in Washington, yet they make up 17% of the children in care. American Indian children (2% of the child population) make up 9% of the children in care [Washington State DSHS Children's Administration 1997b]. Both groups have longer lengths of stay than Caucasian children: for example, 20% of African American children and 22% of American Indian children are in the system for more than four years, compared to 12% of Caucasian children [English & Clark 1996].

Over a two-year period, FFK released several rounds of publications. Questions were raised during presentations that informed the next stages of analysis, helped direct the formulation of strategies for change, and helped identify key issues. Similar to the transformation processes used in corporations, FFK used its key messages to create a sense of urgency and to justify its use of targeted strategies and limited resources to address the problem areas [Kotter 1995]. Presentation of the findings to a wide range of audiences was fundamental to the development of a broad-based coalition necessary to effect system change. Audiences included all levels of DSHS administration, social workers, legislators, judges, the attorney general, tribal councils and American Indian communities, African American communities, child advocates, court-appointed special advocates, and private agencies. Succinct yet powerful messages were created specifically for top leadership to engage their commitment.

Another dissemination tactic used was the repetition of clear, focused messages via presentations, newsletters, news media, public forums, articles, participation in work groups, meetings with key individuals, and broad distribution of FFK reports. In all cases, the messages were kept clear and focused so that the data would remain accessible and meaningful. The demand for this information indicated a desire for constructive data in child welfare, especially localized data.

Data can be easy to ignore and discount—especially when they carry a daunting message. Because FFK's data were often difficult to hear and accept, it was essential that the dissemination strategies used prevented the discounting of the findings and immobilization in the face of enormous challenges. To facilitate receptivity to the findings, FFK placed the data in as local a context as possible. Disbelief about the credibility of the findings was redirected into responsibility at local levels to examine data collection and entry processes. FFK also encouraged and supported further exploration and challenges by the field where possible.

The data presentations were accompanied with a framework for solutions: the findings were not used to dump problems on the system, but explicit solutions were not provided. This framework gave local offices the latitude to formulate solutions that best fit their clients and practice environment, yet provided a structure within which to explore further the issues raised and enough direction to prevent hopelessness from settling in.

Focusing Change Efforts

Strategies for system change needed to (1) be broadly defined yet fit within FFK's focus on permanence; (2) be feasible without a huge infusion of resources; (3) avoid complexity; and (4) offer the highest level of impact. FFK compiled numerous reports that collectively proposed more than 125 recommendations for reform. To sort through these recommendations and determine which strategies would have the highest level of impact, several permanency work groups used a matrix to plot the level of impact (on a horizontal axis) against the level of difficulty for implementation (largely a function of resource availability) along a vertical axis. FFK sought strategies that fit the 80:20 rule: Which few, key strategies could provide the greatest return, or have the most impact [Brocka & Brocka 1992]? For example, implementing prognostic staffings within 90 days of placement would have a high impact on length of stay and present a modest degree of difficulty to implement, requiring primarily a redirection of existing resources. Prognostic staffings thus became a primary strategy for FFK.

FFK played a unique role in engaging both leadership and line staff, and in developing and implementing strategies. The case studies that follow demonstrate the use of relevant data to define and prioritize issues and mobilize change.

Case Study #1: Length of Stay Following Termination of Parental Rights

In the initial round of data publication, FFK released the first description of children who were legally free in Washington state. They were younger than most people expected (76% were 10 years old or younger), in care a long time (mean stay = 4.2 years), particularly following termination of parental rights (47% of their accumulated length of stay), and disproportionately African American and American Indian (more so than expected). A one-year update from the original data collection on these children showed that only one-third had legalized adoptions or guardianships. The one-year update made apparent the problem of long lengths of stay following termination of parental rights, as such stays were occurring even for young children who proceeded to adoption (47% of the adopted children entered out-of-home care as infants) [Bodonyi & Kemp 1996; Bodonyi 1997b].

FFK's most effective data dissemination tool, particularly when used with senior leadership, was a simple chart (figure 1). The darker shading of each bar visually conveys that almost half of the length of time children spend in care occurs post-TPR and highlights the even longer lengths of stay for African American and American Indian children. In the initial presentations with DSHS leadership and the FFK statewide steering committee, audiences reacted with surprise and alarm. Because 80% of the children are adopted by their foster parents or relatives, the length of time in care post-TPR brought forth a flood of questions. The DSHS assistant secretary asked what was delaying adoption legalization. Judges asked how this could be happening in their courtrooms without their awareness. The Washington state attorney general asked how court rules and procedures contributed to delays.

Discussions were also held with volunteer court-appointed special advocates (CASAs), caseworkers, legislators, and community members in public forums. Each group speculated on why children would spend almost half their time in care as legal orphans. Several theories came out of these discussions: the cases had paper reviews (rather than in-court hearings) and were repeatedly continued as "in process"; the urgency to complete the permanent plan was seen as less important for children already placed in their permanent families; the CASA was usually taken off the case following TPR; staffing resources were inadequate to complete adoption homestudies and other paperwork even for

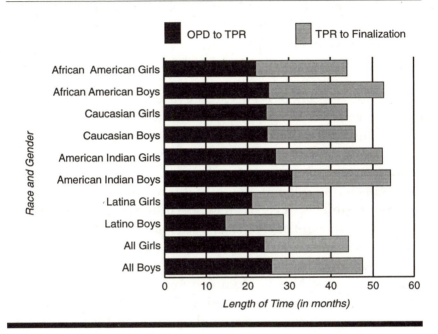

FIGURE 1

Length of Time in Care from Original Placement Date (OPD) to Termination of Parental Rights (TPR) to Adoption Finalization, by Race

foster parent and relative adoptions; and registration of children in need of permanent families and recruitment of families were inadequate.

Faced with the data, each segment of the child welfare system examined how its actions were contributing to the creation of legal orphans, and mobilized action plans statewide within the above systems, including the following changes:

- Judicial reviews with in-court hearings, court case management pilots sponsored by the Court Improvement Project, specialist CASAs for post-TPR cases, and change in appellate court rules to expedite appeals of TPR;
- Legislative allocations of more than $1 million to address the adoption homestudy backlog and the need for coordination of recruitment resources statewide;

- Family unity meetings convened with relatives of legally free children to reexplore biological family connections; and
- A 92% increase in the number of legalized adoptions (from 408 to 785) from 1996 to 1997, and a 111% increase in adoptive placements for children without identified permanent families from 1994 to 1997.

Case Study #2: Infants in Care

A study of 10 years of family foster care and group care placements receiving DSHS payments in Washington state showed that 20% of the children in out-of-home care longer than one year entered care as infants [English & Clark 1996]. In the FFK sample of children in care who were legally free, one-third entered the placement episode in which parental rights were terminated before their first birthdays. Several compelling differences emerged when these findings were analyzed by race that were fundamental to understanding that all children do not move through out-of-home care in the same way. For example, a higher proportion of legally free African American children than legally free children in any other racial/ethnic group entered care as infants (49% compared to 29% of all other children), and 44% of legally free African American infants came directly into care as newborns [Bodonyi 1997a]. Thus, it was apparent that a focus on infants was essential to reduce the disproportionality of African American and American Indian children in care. Further analysis showed that children of all races who entered care as infants had lengths of stay to adoption legalization *just as long* as children of other ages.

The data regarding infants entering out-of-home care and the commensurate strategies for change unfolded over a full year. FFK used two charts to convey the intended messages due to the multiple layers of analysis (figures 2 and 3). The reaction to these findings was a high degree of disbelief and emotion, as the data conflicted with the belief that infants move through care more quickly than children of other ages. At an early presentation, supervisors argued with the presenters that infants may enter care

FIGURE 2

Age at First Placement for Children Who Were Legally Free as of 6/15/95

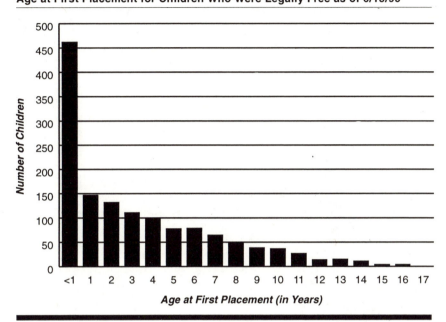

Age at First Placement (in Years)

in higher numbers than children of other ages, but permanent plans are achieved in one to two years. "She just showed you that they stay for years," and "I don't want to believe it's true," were some of the supervisors' responses. That the findings mirrored national data did not increase their credibility, and field workers discounted statewide data by attributing findings to other regions. Once *local* analysis was available, however, social work staff moved from arguments to proposing specific strategies.

In making presentations to DSHS leadership, FFK proposed adapting an existing policy on prognostic staffings that had only been sporadically implemented to date. Once the decision was made to move ahead with this strategy, findings were reintroduced to managers and line staff within the context of prognostic staffings to create a sense of urgency for implementation. FFK believed that, by focusing the state's resources on the youngest

FIGURE 3

Length of Time from Original Placement Date to Adoption Finalization or Guardianship for Children First Placed in Care as Infants (N = 214)

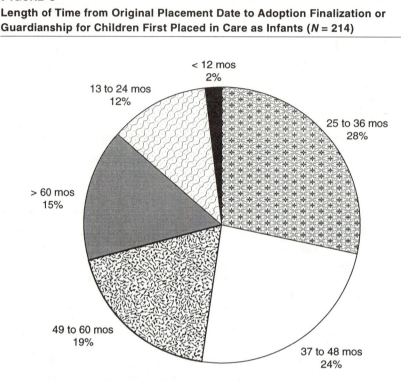

children, the greatest proportion of children entering care would be impacted. Staffings were to be completed 60 days after initial placement, because data showed that children in care longer than 60 days were likely to remain in care for long periods of time [English & Clark 1996]. In addition, as a practical matter, it would be possible in most offices to complete staffings for all of the young children within current resources. Key components of permanency planning, such as identification of children with American Indian ancestry, relative searches, and a concurrent plan should the child not be able to return home, formed the backbone of the staffings. Prognostic staffings have the potential to shift the focus on the early stages of a case rather than the end and thus shorten overall length of time in care.

Confronted with the post-TPR data (case study #1), each stakeholder could easily identify how he or she could institutionalize changes to impact the data. With the racial disproportionality and infant length of stay data, however, proposed solutions became more complex and of necessity moved to front-end decision-making practices.

FFK's data are now widely accepted as part of the knowledge body. By using the same data and basic messages with all stakeholders, all systems can now focus on how they help or hinder children with regard to a permanent family. The field is recognizing the links between infants entering care and children who are legally free—and the interdependence among strategies that impact each end of the system. There is ownership of issues by administrators and social workers. Data dissemination is occurring within different fields through various channels. As the initial surprise and alarm shift to urgency and commitment to action, the challenge is to keep the focus and momentum going.

Practice-Oriented Feedback Mechanisms

A great deal of national attention and fiscal incentives are being placed on establishing systems to gather child welfare data. Plentiful data, however, do not guarantee relevant policy development nor an impact on practice. The child welfare field must develop ongoing feedback mechanisms so that shifts in the client base, practice environment, and children's experiences in out-of-home care can be tracked as they occur, and so that the field, accustomed to responding to changes identified in the data, can make the appropriate changes to continue to deliver effective services. The use of data to create feedback mechanisms differs from the more traditional use of research findings to inform practice. Such findings are often outdated by the time they reach the field and thus have a delayed impact on practice, if any at all.

Several national entities, such as the U.S. Department of Health and Human Services, have been deriving benchmarks for child welfare performance around the issues of safety, child well-being, and permanence. For example, Washington State DSHS has developed the following permanency benchmarks:

- *Placement stability.* The proportion of children with fewer than three placements (homes) during an episode in care.
- *Timely permanency planning.* A high proportion of children with short lengths of time to adoption, guardianship, or reunification.
- *Permanence of completed plan.* A high proportion of children without reentry into care [Washington DSHS Children's Administration 1997a].

Regional and local levels have baseline data and have set benchmark targets for improvement. Their quarterly reports will be used by supervisors, reported to the secretary of DSHS, and be part of the annual report to the governor. Such accountability allows necessary adjustments to be made at multiple levels: practice at the local level, policy development at the regional and state level, and resource allocation at all levels. In this way, data and feedback loops are meaningful from the line worker to top administrators.

The Office of the Attorney General has initiated an audit of all TPR cases statewide and set up a tracking system for these cases. The audit will identify obstacles to timely permanence, which, when remedied, will improve the movement of cases through the courts. This system will also provide ongoing feedback on a local level regarding the progression of TPR cases, allowing trends in practice to be monitored and necessary changes to be initiated without delay.

Conclusion

The integration of data, policy, and fieldwork is essential to system change. FFK used data to create a sense of urgency for change, to focus reform efforts to maximize the use of resources, and to facilitate the development of data-based feedback mechanisms for continuous improvement of practice. The power of the data lies in their relevance to the stated goals, their simplicity, and their ability to be meaningful and localized. It is not only the collection of data, then, but also the thoughtful and judicious use of specific findings that must guide policy. To move beyond resistance, data dissemination tactics must be formulated to mobilize leadership, maximize ownership, and inspire a commitment to action. The data analysis and distillation processes—and the opportunity for research and the field to inform one another—are as essential as the data interpretation and dissemination process. Data brokering is a crucial role that must be integrated into public child welfare for the field to be adequately prepared for the changing trends it will experience in the next century.◆

References

Barth, R. P. (1997). Effects of age and race on the odds of adoption versus remaining in long-term out-of-home care. *Child Welfare, 76,* 285–308.

Bodonyi, J. (1997a). *Age at first placement and length of stay in care: Findings on infants in care and the disproportionality of African American and Native American children.* Seattle, WA: Families for Kids.

Bodonyi, J. (1997b). *One year update on legally free children in Washington State: Revisiting the status of children who were legally free as of June 15, 1995.* Seattle, WA: Families for Kids.

Bodonyi, J., & Kemp, S. (1996). *Characteristics of legally free children and recommendations for permanency in Washington State.* Seattle, WA: Families for Kids.

Brocka, B., & Brocka, M. S. (1992). *Quality management: Implementing the best ideas of the masters.* Homewood, IL: Business One Irving.

Courtney, M. E., & Collins, R. C. (1994). New challenges and opportunities in child welfare outcomes and information technologies. *Child Welfare, 73,* 359–378.

English, D., & Clark, T. (1996). *Report of children in foster and group care placements in Washington State between June 1985 and August 1995.* Seattle, WA: Washington State Division of Children and Family Services, Office of Children's Administration Research.

Goerge, R. M., Wulczyn, F. H., & Harden, A. W. (1994). *A report from the Multistate Foster Care Data Archive: Foster care dynamics, 1983–1992.* Chicago: University of Chicago, Chapin Hall Center for Children.

Kotter, J. P. (1995). Leading change: Why transformation efforts fail. *Harvard Business Review, 73*(2), 59–67.

Spar, K. (1997). *Foster care and adoption statistics.* Washington, DC: Congressional Research Service.

Washington State Department of Social and Health Services, Children's Administration (1997a). *Benchmarks in permanency: Initial report.* Olympia, WA: Management Services Division, Division of Program and Policy.

Washington State Department of Social and Health Services, Children's Administration (1997b). *CAMIS key indicators 1997 quarterly reports.* Olympia, WA: Management Services Division, Division of Program and Policy.

Measuring Performance in Child Welfare: Secondary Effects of Success

2

Charles L. Usher, Judith B. Wildfire, and
Deborah A. Gibbs

The Adoption and Safe Families Act of 1997 mandates the development of a system to rate the performance of state child welfare programs. The resulting system, built on broader efforts to measure outcomes for children and families who receive support and services from the child welfare system, will inform perspectives on family foster care in the next century. Drawing on findings from evaluations of recent reform initiatives in Alabama, North Carolina, and Ohio, this article suggests that performance measurement systems must be adaptable to changing circumstances, particularly when improvements in one area can affect standards and expectations in others.

Charles L. Usher, Ph.D., is Wallace H. Kuralt Senior Professor of Public Welfare, School of Social Work, University of North Carolina at Chapel Hill, Chapel Hill, NC. Judith B. Wildfire, M.P.A., M.P.H., is Clinical Instructor, Jordan Institute for Families, University of North Carolina at Chapel Hill, Chapel Hill, NC. Deborah A. Gibbs, M.P.H., is Research Analyst, Research Triangle Institute, Research Triangle Park, NC. This research was supported by grants from the Annie E. Casey Foundation and the W.K. Kellogg Foundation, and by contracts with the North Carolina Department of Health and Human Services. The opinions and conclusions expressed here are those of the authors and are not necessarily shared by the sponsors.

Concerns about the well-being of children in out-of-home care have led to a variety of efforts to reform the child welfare system. Over the past 20 years, federal legislation has produced the policy framework known as permanency planning [Adoption Assistance and Child Welfare Act of 1980, P.L. 96-272], new financial resources for family preservation and support services [Omnibus Budget Reconciliation Act of 1993, P.L. 103–66], and most recently, a national commitment to move more children from out-of-home care into adoptive homes [Adoption and Safe Families Act of 1997, P.L. 105–89]. At the state and local level, efforts to bring about change have come in three forms: (1) consent decrees arising from legal actions advocates have brought in the courts [e.g., R.C. v. Hornsby 1991]; (2) reform initiatives embarked on by governors, child welfare leaders, and other stakeholders [Usher et al. 1995]; and (3) demonstration programs authorized by waivers of federal regulations based on Title IV-E of the Social Security Act, under which state out-of-home care programs obtain federal funding.

Unfortunately, a recent assessment by the U.S. General Accounting Office concluded that "[a]lthough initiatives are in place, most… states have not systematically evaluated the impact of them, and data concerning these efforts [are] limited" [U.S. GAO 1997: 3]. A number of factors contributes to this lack of information. A subtle obstacle may be an organizational culture within child welfare agencies that discourages performance measurement for fear that additional data will fuel attacks from the system's detractors, who evaluate performance "more on the basis of tragedies than successes" [Vincent 1997: 19]. A recent series of focus groups with frontline workers suggest that the perceptions of those closest to practice may be dominated by the tremendous difficulty of the work and by a strong sense that their efforts lack support from the public, policymakers, and management [Gibbs 1997].

Continued reliance on measures based on point-in-time data

also obscures improvements in outcomes. In spite of repeated warnings that they are biased toward the experience of children who have the worst experience with the child welfare system (e.g., Usher et al. [1995]; Wulczyn [1996]), data based on snapshots of child welfare caseloads continue to be used inappropriately by many child welfare administrators, policymakers, advocates, and some researchers. Even the Adoption and Foster Care Analysis and Reporting System (AFCARS) established by the federal Administration for Children and Families falls prey to this problem. The pessimistic perspective created by these data has made the challenge of improving the performance of child welfare agencies seem so daunting that those seeking change have tended to ignore the possibility that their efforts might actually succeed.

Results emerging from two child welfare reform efforts, the Family to Family initiative sponsored by the Annie E. Casey Foundation, and the Families for Kids initiative sponsored by the W.K. Kellogg Foundation, as well as anecdotal information from the U.S. General Accounting Office, indicate that significant improvements are, in fact, being made [U.S. GAO 1997]. Cognizant of repeated failures to measure the impact of reform efforts, the foundations sponsoring these initiatives insisted that the states and localities partnering with them accede to rigorous evaluation. The federal government also is imposing the same requirement on states conducting demonstration programs under Title IV-E waivers. Thus, claims of success now have a stronger foundation.

The performance measurement system called for in the Adoption and Safe Families Act of 1997 is an outgrowth of the attention that has been given to measuring outcomes for children and families who receive support and services from the child welfare system. The resulting system will inform perspectives on out-of-home care in the next century and create the framework that defines good performance. Therefore, it should draw on recent experience in evaluating child welfare programs and in establishing outcome-based performance systems.

This article presents selected results from the evaluations of the Family to Family and Families for Kids reform initiatives. Although the approaches of these two efforts are different (see Usher et al. [1995]), they share certain objectives, including lowering the number of children entering or reentering out-of-home care, making out-of-home care less restrictive and less disruptive, and reducing lengths of stay. Additionally, data from the evaluation of Family to Family in Alabama make it possible to assess the new system of care being created under the consent decree in *R.C. v. Hornsby* [1991].*

Evaluation Framework

The evaluation strategy pursued in the six states involved in the Family to Family initiative and in North Carolina's Families for Kids initiative diverges from conventional evaluative approaches in important ways. First, by merging self-evaluation principles with nonequivalent comparison group designs, it assesses progress toward the initiative's goals by tracking and comparing outcomes in comparable localities or neighborhoods (see Usher [1995]). In North Carolina, for example, the comparison is being drawn between eight counties selected to implement the Families for Kids initiative and the state's remaining 92 counties. In Alabama, outcomes for children entering care in the first group of counties in which the *R.C.* consent decree was implemented are contrasted with other groups of counties as the entire state converts in stages to a new system of care. Implementation and comparison sites in both states provided planning data about the experiences of children who entered out-of-home care in the years preceding implementation. These data also provided a baseline for evaluating changes in outcomes during the initiative.

---

* Under the terms of the consent decree, the Alabama Department of Human Resources agreed to implement a new "system of care" according to a strict schedule. The decree enunciated specific operational principles, such as the development of individual needs-based service plans (ISPs) and active involvement of family members in developing the plan.

The second way in which the evaluations of these initiatives differ from conventional approaches is in their emphasis on the use of longitudinal data. These data describe the experiences of successive cohorts of children who initially entered out-of-home care over a series of years encompassing a preimplementation period and extending throughout implementation of the initiative (see Usher et al. [1995]). Derived from existing child welfare information systems, these data provide placement histories for children entering out-of-home care for the first time during a given 12-month period, typically a calendar or fiscal year. These statistical case histories encompass the experiences of children in care from their initial date of custody and their first placement in out-of-home care, through all subsequent placements, and finally, to their exit from the child welfare system. The system's continuing follow-up also captures reentries into care for children who come back into out-of-home care following permanent placement at the end of their first out-of-home care experience.

Although the Family to Family and Families for Kids initiatives emphasize some of the same outcomes, each has distinctive features requiring appropriate outcome measures and analytical methods. At the core of Family to Family is an effort to build a neighborhood-based out-of-home care system that draws on and enhances the informal and formal resources located near children who must enter out-of-home care. The local child welfare agency seeks to partner with neighborhood residents to ensure the safety and well-being of children by expanding family supports and foster care resources. In addition, the initiative recognizes that changes in frontline practice are constrained by policy and management, and therefore, calls for changes in legislation, regulation, financing, and program structure that will reinforce practice changes (see Usher et al. [1995]).

The improvements sought by Family to Family include reducing the number of children entering out-of-home care, using less restrictive placements (such as kinship care), minimizing disruptions while in care, shortening lengths of stay, increasing the rate of reunification and other forms of permanent placements, and avoiding reentry into care for children following the achievement of a permanent placement at the end of the initial experience in out-of-home care. In some cases, Family to Family has been implemented in conjunction with a broader initiative, usually undertaken by the governor, to improve outcomes for families. In Alabama, state officials saw it as a mutually reinforcing complement to the R.C. consent decree they had negotiated in the preceding year with plaintiffs in a suit against the state.

The Families for Kids initiative in North Carolina, similar to initiatives the Kellogg Foundation sponsored in other states, emphasized reducing the "backlog" of children who remained in out-of-home care longer than one year and for whom it had been difficult to find a permanent home. The initiative focused on five changes in approach: comprehensive family support; one caseworker or casework team for each case; a single assessment to determine needs; a single foster family prior to permanent placement; and a maximum of one year to achieve a permanent placement. Assessing progress toward these objectives, like those in Family to Family, required longitudinal data, but also involved special performance measures, such as tracking rates of exit from care for children who remained in custody 12 months after entering care.

Progress toward outcomes in both initiatives has been assessed with descriptive analytic methods, as well as survival analysis techniques appropriate for estimating the length of time children remain in out-of-home care. Qualitative data, collected by means of focus groups with foster care workers and foster parents in both implementation and comparison sites in the Family to Family states, were used to supplement the longitudinal data.*

---

* Led by a trained moderator, 40 focus groups of 8 to 12 participants were conducted in five Family to Family sites.

Findings

The examples below use data from Alabama, Ohio, and North Carolina and are based on the experiences of 18,104 children who entered care in Alabama between October 1, 1988, and September 30, 1996, including 2,305 children from the group of counties involved in the initial stage of implementing the *R.C.* consent decree (termed Stage 1 counties); 12,653 children who entered out-of-home care in Cuyahoga County, Ohio, from 1990 through 1996; and 29,031 children who entered out-of-home care in North Carolina between July 1, 1991, and March 31, 1997.

The data documenting the children's experiences in out-of-home care were extracted from administrative databases normally used to track out-of-home care custody status and payments. The validity and reliability of these data are better than survey recall in terms of the specific type of placement that a child experienced and the exact duration of each placement. The case records of children in out-of-home care are subject to audit and federal review, an oversight process that encourages accuracy in recording. Also, given that items such as the date of placement and the type of placement determine payments to providers, and that inaccurate information is likely to prompt a complaint from a provider, caseworkers have compelling reasons to enter data accurately.

Alabama

In 1991, the Division of Child and Family Services in Alabama embarked upon an ambitious reform of the state's child welfare system. Under the so-called *R.C.* consent decree negotiated by the plaintiffs and the Alabama Department of Human Resources, the state agreed to implement a new system for out-of-home care over a period of several years. Formal implementation of the reforms began early in 1992 with a group of counties designated as Stage 1 counties. Later that year, Alabama received a grant from

FIGURE 1

Number of Children Entering Out-of-Home Care in Stage 1 and Preconversion Counties

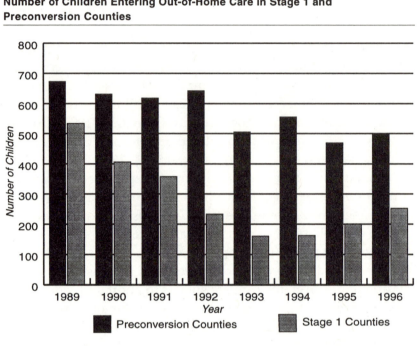

the Annie E. Casey Foundation to participate in Family to Family, the objectives of which were seen as entirely consistent with those of the *R.C.* consent decree, and therefore, mutually reinforcing.

The objectives of the consent decree and Family to Family span several areas: reducing the number of children entering out-of-home care; speeding reunification; and establishing permanency for children for whom out-of-home care is the only alternative. The early attainment of these goals is evident in both figures 1 and 2. Although there was a steady decline over the years in the number of children entering out-of-home care in the preconversion counties, the reduction never reached the dimensions that it did in the Stage 1 counties. In 1989, about 530 children entered out-of-home care for the first time in the Stage 1 counties compared to 670 in the preconversion counties. By 1993,

FIGURE 2
Lengths of Stay in Alabama

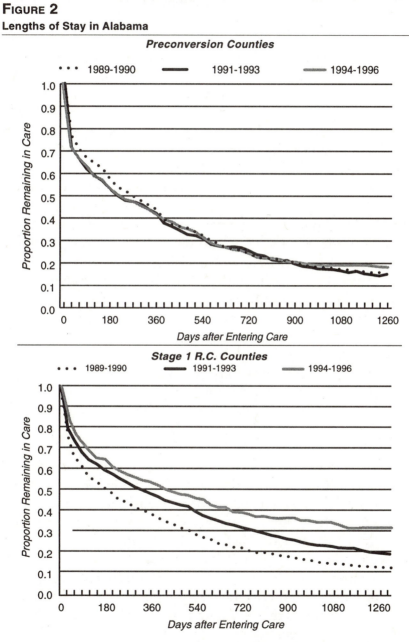

Preconversion Counties

• • • 1989-1990   ━━━ 1991-1993   ▨▨▨ 1994-1996

Proportion Remaining in Care

Days after Entering Care

Stage 1 R.C. Counties

• • • 1989-1990   ━━━ 1991-1993   ▨▨▨ 1994-1996

Proportion Remaining in Care

Days after Entering Care

well into the conversion process, the number of children entering care in the Stage 1 counties had declined by 65% to fewer than 150, compared to a 26% decrease to 500 in the preconversion counties. Beginning in 1994, however, the number of children entering care in Stage 1 counties began to increase.

Similarly, figure 2 shows an initial improvement in the length of time that children remained in out-of-home care. In the early years of conversion (1991 to 1993), the median length of stay for children in Stage 1 counties was approximately six months, compared to just under one year for children who entered care prior to implementation of the system of care required by the consent decree (1989 to 1990). In more recent years, however, the median length of time that children spend in out-of-home care has increased significantly (to more than 400 days), surpassing the median for the years prior to the beginning of the consent decree. Consistent with this finding, the proportion of children who are still in care after one year, two years, and three years has increased. At each time point, the pattern is the same—the largest proportion of children still in care is seen in the later conversion years (1994–1996) and the smallest proportion is seen in the early conversion years. In the preconversion counties there was virtually no change in the time that children spent in out-of-home care for children in all eight annual cohorts.

Ohio

As table 1 shows, the number of children initially entering out-of-home care in Cuyahoga County varied widely from 1990 to 1996. In 1990, just over 1,400 children entered out-of-home care for the first time. The number grew substantially in 1991, but declined in 1992 and 1993 before rising again in 1994. This was followed by a decrease in 1995; in 1996, however, Cuyahoga County experienced its largest increase in children entering care, as the number of children entering care jumped to over 2,500.

Figure 3 clarifies the changing pattern of admissions that is masked by the fluctuation in raw numbers in table 1. The chart

TABLE 1

Number of Children Entering Care for First Time, by Year and Type of Initial Placement

Initial Placement	1990	1991	1992	1993	1994	1995	1996
Agency Foster Home	358	464	363	377	412	314	413
Network Foster Home	96	204	197	239	364	348	309
Relative	317	609	617	634	814	739	1423
Public Children's Residential Center	110	92	79	6	—	—	—
Private Children's Residential Center	64	61	45	31	72	49	57
Group Home	55	50	30	11	28	20	24
Hospital	77	99	94	57	52	53	111
Other	347	352	346	165	125	102	178
Total	1424	1931	1771	1520	1867	1625	2515

shows changes in at least three areas. First, the proportion of children initially placed in relatively more restrictive settings, such as children's residential centers (including the county's emergency shelter) and group homes, declined significantly. In fact, the county shelter was converted to a reunification center in 1993 as one of the initial changes associated with Family to Family. Second, as a result of negotiations with private providers, children were stepped down in care from group homes to private "network" family foster homes, and providers began to establish foster homes in target neighborhoods from which many children were being removed for placement. Third, the proportion of children placed with relatives grew from less than one-fourth to more than half. The substantial increase in admissions in 1996 was absorbed almost entirely by such placements, and as discussed below, resulted from deliberate changes in county policies.

North Carolina

An integral feature of the Families for Kids initiative has been its emphasis on reducing the "backlog" of children in the out-of-home care system. When state leaders and leaders in eight coun-

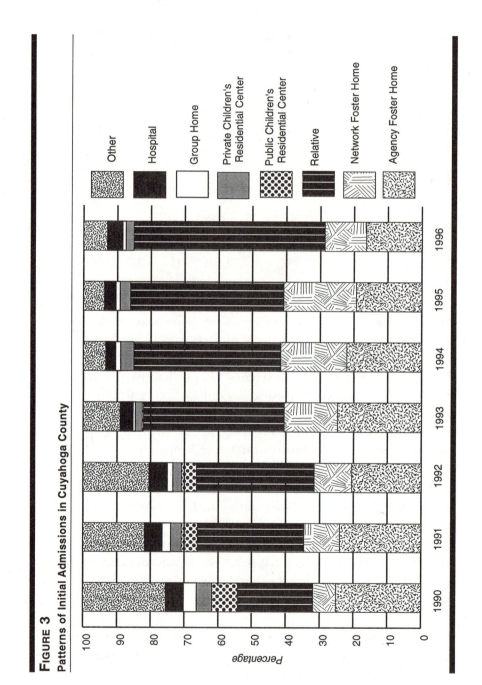

FIGURE 3
Patterns of Initial Admissions in Cuyahoga County

ties in North Carolina embarked on the initiative, they chose to define the backlog in the state as encompassing any child who remained in care longer than 12 months. In contrast to some other Families for Kids grantees, North Carolina's reform efforts give equal emphasis to avoiding the movement of children *into* the backlog as to removing children *from* the backlog. It is in this context that North Carolina grantees view the initiative as an opportunity for systemic reform rather than as a "project" to eliminate a backlog.

To increase awareness of the status of each child relative to the initiative's goals, participating counties received information about rates of exit from care and patterns of care experienced by children who had entered care in the three years prior to the start of Families for Kids. This enabled participants in North Carolina to identify when children were most likely to leave care or to linger without much chance of exit. Using these data as a baseline, caseworkers and supervisors were sensitized to the status of children currently in care (and those entering care) and encouraged to take steps to avoid the entry of children into the backlog.

As figure 4 shows, the survival curves for the FY 1994 cohort indicate a small difference in the length of stay of children placed with relatives in the Families for Kids counties compared to those who entered care that year in other counties (the curves are virtually identical for the FY 1993 cohorts). Among children who entered care and were placed with relatives in FY 1995, the median length of time in placement authority remained just under 18 months (540 days) for children from counties not part of Families for Kids. In contrast, children entering care in Families for Kids counties tended to leave care much sooner, with a median length of stay of just over one year. Also, whereas nearly half the children who entered care in nonparticipating counties were still in care after 18 months, just over one-fourth of the children from Families for Kids counties remained in care that long.

The marked change in the slope of the survival curve for the

FIGURE 4

Lengths of Stay for Children Placed with Relatives in North Carolina

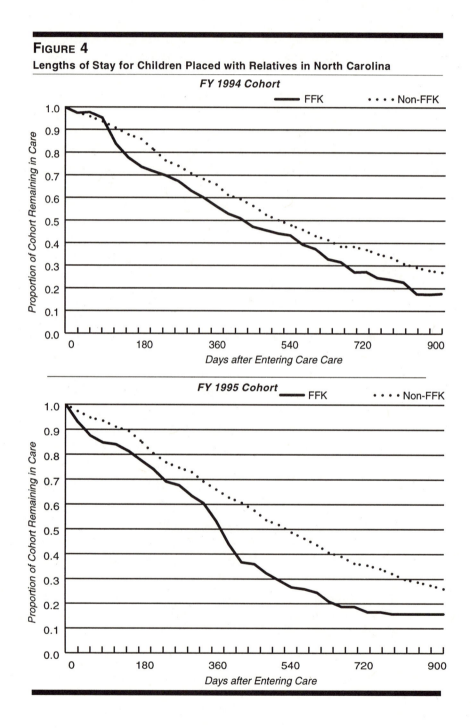

FY 1994 Cohort

— FFK   • • • • Non-FFK

Proportion of Cohort Remaining in Care

Days after Entering Care Care

FY 1995 Cohort

— FFK   • • • • Non-FFK

Proportion of Cohort Remaining in Care

Days after Entering Care

FY 1995 cohort of children from Families for Kids counties indicates the effort of agencies in those counties to conform to the "one year to permanency" outcome promulgated by the initiative. In the month leading up to the one-year mark and in the two succeeding months, the proportion of children remaining in care declined by nearly 40%, from just over 0.6 to approximately 0.37. Consistent with this, the hazard rates associated with these monthly intervals (indicating the likelihood of exiting care during a given interval) are substantially higher than those for the preceding or succeeding intervals. As discussed below, however, these changes did not seem to affect reentry rates.

Discussion

The findings presented in this article suggest that child welfare program operations changed because of these initiatives, and with those changes, the experiences of children entering out-of-home care in these states and communities changed as well. Trends within target communities point to change, and the conclusion that change actually occurred is reinforced by data suggesting that outcomes for children in comparison communities did not undergo similar changes. Examination of the three illustrations helps explain the changes indicated by the charts and other data.

Alabama

The results for Alabama are interesting in that the impact of the R.C. consent decree was not apparent from the caseload data being used by court monitors. By focusing on a succession of cohorts of children entering the system and by describing their subsequent experiences, the longitudinal data show the extent to which entries to care and lengths of stay were reduced—and later rose. The impact of changes called for by the consent decree, as intended, was most apparent for children entering out-of-home care and for those at risk of entering care.

Certain aspects of the Alabama findings should be noted. First, by focusing on alternatives to out-of-home care and reducing length of stay, the state achieved quick and substantial reductions in the number of children entering care and reduced lengths of stay for those for whom placement outside the home was the only alternative. The magnitude of these reductions suggests that the opportunities for change were not difficult to identify.

Eventually, however, a lower limit seems to have been reached. At this point, according to the authors' discussions with local child welfare staff, the children entering care were more likely to be those with significant needs, and thus, those who would (as the data indicate) experience longer lengths of stay. Also, after a period of aggressive efforts to reduce entries into out-of-home care, the subsequent rise in placements suggests a period of readjustment in which there was more confidence that such resources could be used without again becoming overly reliant on them. The results from Ohio show a similar phenomenon at work.

Ohio

The findings for Cuyahoga County also reveal a system undergoing substantial changes. A new county administration and a commitment to the Family to Family initiative first brought changes in 1992 and 1993. The closing of the shelter and a clearly enunciated shift away from congregate care facilities were the first indications of these changes, along with the discontinuation of placements with "unrelated individuals," that is, unlicensed friends and neighbors who cared for children under the protection of the county (included in the "Other" category in table 1). These changes were accompanied by a new emphasis on placements with relatives, a placement option that now accounts for more than half of all initial placements.

In moving away from congregate care, the new administration sought to establish a different relationship with private providers under which additional network family foster homes would be established in neighborhoods where children were being removed from their homes. In response to a request for proposals, several providers formed community collaboratives with neighborhood centers and moved in this direction. Also, recognizing the shift in policy, other providers made adjustments to accommodate in family foster homes children who formerly would have been placed in group homes or other congregate care facilities.

The dramatic increase in children entering out-of-home care in 1996 was prompted by several factors, but largely reflects conscious choices to bring more children into care, in great part due to increased reliance on kinship care. Consistent with a perceived increase in the number of drug-exposed infants, table 1 shows an increase in the number of children in hospitals when they entered care. Along with this phenomenon, however, was recognition that many of these infants had older siblings whose safety and well-being also might be at risk. As a result, more sibling groups entered child welfare custody, but many were handled through kinship care arrangements. As table 1 indicates, the number of placements to family foster homes and other settings did not increase substantially and may have actually declined in 1996.

Partly as a result of a review of a sample of family preservation cases, Cuyahoga County also introduced new guidelines for risk-assessment screening in 1996. In the context of several highly publicized child fatalities, these guidelines were seen by some staff as encouraging placement outside the home. Although the agency had introduced "family team meetings" as a process for making placement and permanency decisions, the guidelines seemed to heighten awareness of the risks facing children who come to the agency's attention. This awareness, and the exposure workers felt as a result of critical publicity, almost certainly contributed to the increase in entries to care.

North Carolina

The results from the Families for Kids initiative in North Carolina are a testament to the importance of the messages conveyed in a reform process. The concept of the "backlog" and the goal of achieving permanency for all children within one year of their entry to out-of-home care could be easily communicated to a wide range of stakeholders—social workers, judges, elected officials, and families. It thus became a standard against which to assess the progress an agency was making with each child in its care.

The longitudinal data developed in this initiative were essential in the application by the eight counties of the performance standard that had been established in principle during the planning phase. The underlying notion of tracking the experience of every child who entered care and assessing his or her progress toward permanency had intuitive appeal. After obtaining baseline data describing the experience of children who had come into their care in the four years prior to the start of Families for Kids, the eight counties implementing the initiative had a context within which to assess the results of their efforts. In smaller agencies, this amounted simply to identifying, on a spreadsheet, every child in out-of-home care and having monthly reviews to evaluate each child's progress toward the goal of avoiding entry into the backlog or leaving it.

In contrast to the relatively more mature initiatives in Alabama and Ohio, Families for Kids in North Carolina is just reaching the point at which it is possible to assess unintended consequences. Although the initiative seems to have affected the rate and pattern of exits from care, the question remains as to whether the decisions being made will ultimately be in the best interests of children and their families. By linking data for all placements children experience, it is possible to track rates of reentry to care following a permanent placement. A comparison of reentry rates for children who entered care in Families for Kids counties with children who entered care in other counties does not reveal significant differences. In fact, reentry rates for children entering care in the eight counties involved in the initiative are slightly lower and the difference has increased in the years following implementation of the initiative. Acknowledging the need for earlier recognition of signs of re-abuse, however, state officials are building the capacity to monitor rates of substantiated reports of abuse and neglect for children who leave out-of-home care.

Conclusions

Section 203 of P.L. 105-89, the Adoption and Safe Families Act of 1997, calls for the U.S. Department of Health and Human Services to "develop a set of outcome measures (including length of stay in foster care, number of foster care placements, and number of adoptions) that can be used to assess the performance of states in operating child protection and child welfare programs." The results emerging from the evaluations of the three initiatives described here provide lessons for the development of such a performance measurement system.

The basic pattern of outcomes observed in the reform sites described here include substantial reductions in the number of children entering out-of-home care compared to a multiyear baseline period and to similar nonreform localities in the same state. This reduction in entry into care was often accompanied by a reduced reliance on relatively more restrictive placement settings. Some sites in both initiatives also were able to reduce lengths of stay and disruptions in care. These accomplishments are noteworthy in and of themselves, but the multiyear timeframe of the initiatives made it possible also to see the emergence of certain secondary effects.

One aspect of the secondary effect of reform is that the children entering care in the second stage are different from those who entered care in the prereform period, and better outcomes for these second stage children are not as easily achieved. In the second stage of reform in some sites, lengths of stay rose to levels similar to the prereform period or to those experienced by children in nonreform sites. For these children, however, longer lengths of stay are more likely to be related to the needs of the children rather than to inattention by the system. In a few cases, the number of children entering care for the first time also increased, apparently as a result of an adjustment in standards of admission that had been applied in the initial stage of reform.

Another secondary effect of reform is that participants are able to learn from their experiences. Officials in Alabama first saw the effects of the consent decree in the longitudinal data. Cuyahoga County administrators revised their risk assessment guidelines based on what they learned about family preservation cases. North Carolina agency staff obtained a new perspective on the status of children in their care by tracking them against explicit outcome-oriented standards. In each case, there was an increased awareness of change and of the direction it was taking. The result was not only a greater sense of control, but also a recognition of the need to monitor and respond to ongoing changes.

The results of these initiatives are encouraging in that they demonstrate that improvements in performance are possible. They also suggest a need for caution, however, in adopting a few simplistic performance indicators and ignoring changes in context that dictate adjustments in performance standards and expectations. The accomplishment of one set of goals (e.g., reduced admissions) can have repercussions on other performance indicators (e.g., length of stay). Systems for monitoring and evaluating the performance of child welfare systems must acknowledge these interdependencies.

Increasingly, the components of comprehensive and sophisticated performance measurement are being at least partially put into place. A growing number of agencies are using longitudinal analytic techniques, and databases that make it possible to track cohorts of children entering the system are well-established in an increasing number of states [e.g., Barth et al. 1994; Goerge et al. 1994; Usher et al. 1996]. The experience of recent efforts, however, suggests that monitoring a few measures is unlikely to provide a full and accurate assessment of the performance of child welfare systems. The constantly changing environment in which these systems operate requires an evolutionary approach to performance measurement that anticipates change and is able to respond to it. Self-evaluation and performance teams such as those used in these initiatives provide a means for continually updating performance expectations as well as monitoring progress toward desired outcomes.◆

References

Adoption and Safe Families Act of 1997, P.L. No. 105–89 (1997).

Adoption Assistance and Child Welfare Act of 1980, P.L. No. 96–272 (1980).

Barth, R. P., Courtney, M., Berrick, J. D., & Albert, V. (1994). *From child abuse to permanency planning: Child welfare services pathways and placements.* New York: Aldine de Gruyter.

Gibbs, D. A. (1997). *Implementing change in child welfare: Lessons from Family to Family.* Research Triangle Park, NC: Research Triangle Institute.

Goerge, R. M., Wulczyn, F. H., & Harden, A. W. (1994). *Foster care dynamics 1983–1992: A report from the Multistate Foster Care Data Archive.* Chicago: University of Chicago, The Chapin Hall Center for Children.

Omnibus Budget Reconciliation Act of 1993, P.L. No. 103–66 (1993).

R.C. v. Hornsby, No. 88–H–1170–N (M.D. Al. May 1991).

U.S. General Accounting Office. (1997, May). *Foster care: State efforts to improve the permanency planning process show some promise.* Report to the Chairman, Subcommittee on Human Resources, Committee on Ways and Means, House of Representatives, GAO/HEHS–97–73.

Usher, C. L. (1995). Improving evaluability through self–evaluation. *Evaluation Practice, 16,* 55–64.

Usher, C. L., Gibbs, D. A., Gogan, H. C., & Wildfire, J. B. (1996). *Measuring outcomes in child welfare: Lessons from Family to Family.* Research Triangle Park, NC: Research Triangle Institute.

Usher, C. L., Gibbs, D. A., & Wildfire, J. B. (1995). A framework for planning, implementing and evaluating child welfare reforms. *Child Welfare, 74,* 859–876.

Vincent, P. (1997). The organizational culture of child protective services. *Family Resource Coalition Report, 16*(2), 19–22.

Wulczyn, F. (1996). Note on research: A statistical and methodological framework for analyzing the foster care experiences of children. *Social Service Review, 70,* 319–329.

3 Satisfaction of Children in Out-of-Home Care

Leslie Wilson and James Conroy

A randomly selected sample of 1,100 children in out-of-home care in Illinois from 1993 to 1996 were interviewed in person regarding their satisfaction with the homes in which they lived and with their caregivers. They were also asked whether they felt loved and safe, and rated the quality of their lives before and after placement into care. The children rated their satisfaction with their living arrangements and with their caregivers as high, especially those who had lived in family foster care.

Leslie Wilson, M.S., is Project Director, Wilson Resources, Inc., Tallahassee, FL. James Conroy, Ph.D., is Data Analyst and Technical Advisor, The Center for Outcome Analysis, Bryn Mawr, PA.

In 1995, an estimated 486,000 children were living in out-of-home care in America's child welfare systems [Petit et al. 1997]. Despite the increasing number of children in out-of-home care, few studies document their satisfaction with their current homes, the services they are receiving, and the quality of their lives. Those studies that have documented interviews with children were based on small samples of fewer than 60 children [Johnson et al. 1995 (N = 59); Gardner 1996 (N = 51)] or were conducted with children postplacement [Benedict et al. 1996].

A holistic evaluation of the quality of out-of-home care should include interviews with the children. Among the many quality of life outcomes that are measurable, consumer satisfaction is certainly one of the most important. No system can consistently improve unless it receives feedback. As one researcher has said, "The children themselves should be consulted... they are a key source of information that has too often been overlooked" [Dubowitz 1994].

Child welfare systems have popularized the term *empowerment* as they have implemented reforms [Dunlap 1997]. This word is used most often when referring to the children's biological parents or the children's caregivers. Empowerment, however, is also vital to children, since opportunities for self-determination during childhood impact their adult lives. One of the first steps in making children feel empowered is to seek out their input and to value their opinions.

The consistency of the results of the four years of interviews documented in this article reflects the children's ability to report on their own circumstances and assess their own needs. Although children should be considered key members of their permanency planning teams, as their lives are impacted by the judgments adults make, they are frequently neither asked for nor heard when they offer an opinion on the quality of their lives or their dreams for the future.

This article describes selected results from four years of directly asking children in out-of-home care about their lives, level of satisfaction, and preferences.

Background

The four Annual Client Evaluations (ACE) summarized in this article consisted of interviews with 1,100 children in out-of-home care in Illinois' child welfare system during calendar years 1993, 1994, 1995, and 1996. The children were asked about the overall quality of their lives before and after placement, and about their level of satisfaction with their current homes, caregivers, caseworkers, and the services they received from the child welfare agency and its contracted provider agencies. The characteristics of the children were also documented.*

Nearly 86% of the 1,100 children interviewed were living in family foster care, kinship care, or nonrelative care ($n = 942$); 14% of the children were living in residential group care placements (group homes, child care institutions, shelters, or any placement that was not family foster care) ($n = 158$). The living arrangements of the children in the study sample were comparable to those documented by the state child welfare agency's tracking system. In September 1996, the state agency was serving 50,611 children in out-of-home care: 91% of the children were living in family foster care; 9% of the children were living in some type of residential group care [IDCFS 1996]. The percentage of children in family foster care in Illinois was within a few percentage points all four years and reflects the state's emphasis on family foster care in placement decisions. Nationally, approximately 70% of children in out-of-home care are living in family foster homes [Risley-Curtiss 1997].

The ACEs generated satisfaction data as well as demographic information that increased the child welfare agency's knowledge of the children in the out-of-home care system. This information offered policymakers and funders the unique opportunity to review current child welfare practices based on data gleaned from representative samples of children. Such feedback is not only

* The project also involved interviews with each child's biological parents (when available), foster parents, and child care workers. Results of those aspects of the research were reported to the state agency, but are not the topic of the present article.

useful, but a necessity in the current child welfare environment. "Outcome measures are going to be increasingly important in the years ahead. In today's competitive climate, empirical evidence is vital. As budgets get leaner and meaner, and agencies are asked to do more with less, they need to know which services are most effective for which populations" [Child Welfare League of America 1996: 22].

Method

Subjects

This study provides data from interviews with 1,100 children from 1993 through 1996: 250 children were interviewed in 1993, 250 in 1994, 300 in 1995, and 300 in 1996. The children were served by Illinois' child welfare system and were living in out-of-home care, primarily family foster care (86%), at the time they were interviewed. Samples were designed differently and independently in each year of the project; sample selection methods ranged from simple random sampling to the use of stratified sampling.*

The researchers were acting as agents of state government and as such, informed consent was not required. Nevertheless, no child was ever interviewed without requesting permission and receiving oral consent. The interviewers signed statements of confidentiality to protect the privacy of the children and those around them. Interviewers were fully informed during training of the penalties they would face for breaching confidentiality.

Instrument

The researchers reviewed the literature for outcome-oriented instruments [Magura & Moses 1986] and, finding none that met the needs of the present project, designed their own instrument. Issues the state child welfare agency wanted addressed included

---

* Details on each year's sampling process may be obtained from the senior author.

demographic information on the children; the children's satisfaction with various aspects of their lives and services, happiness with where they lived, and self-perceived quality of life before and after placement; and the children's relationships with
the caseworkers, the child welfare agency serving them, the juvenile court, biological family members, other children living in
their homes, and caregivers. The resulting questionnaire con-
tained 49 quantitative questions (close-ended questions with answers given on scales or numbered choices) and seven qualitative questions (open-ended questions with answers taken down
verbatim).* A pilot study was conducted in 1992 to test the instrument. Minor changes in wording and sequence were made
to the survey instrument and full scale application began in 1993.

Data Collection

Interviews with the children were conducted in private in their
homes, unless the children requested that someone other than
the interviewer be present.

The interviewers were professionals with undergraduate and
advanced degrees and experience in the human service field.
Seven of the original 11 interviewers stayed with the project for
three of its four years. In 1995, additional interviewers were added
to meet the expanded number of individuals to be interviewed.
In 1996, the sample was stratified by race/ethnicity and two Span-
ish-speaking interviewers were recruited.

The interviewers received eight hours of training each year
at a centralized location. Training consisted of information on
interviewing techniques and etiquette, procedures for scheduling interviews, handling situations the interviewer considered
dangerous to the child interviewed, and the use of the questionnaires. Training attendance was mandatory.

---

* An example of a quantitative item is: "How do you feel about living here?" (Five-
point scale from "very unhappy" to "very happy.") An example of a qualitative item
is: "If your answer was 'unhappy' or 'very unhappy', why are you unhappy here?"
Copies of the instrument may be obtained from the senior author.

Interviewers were told to rephrase questions to assure the child understood, but not to lead the child toward any specific answer via body language, tonality, or facial expressions. Children were informed that they did not have to be interviewed, that they could stop the interview at anytime, and that whether or not they agreed to be interviewed would have no bearing on their situation.

Interviewers were also instructed to tell the children before the interview began that they were not employees of the child welfare agency and to encourage the children to share with their caseworkers, counselors, caregivers, or relatives the concerns they expressed during the interview.

To help the younger children understand the Likert scales, a response sheet with five faces expressing great happiness, happiness, no emotion, unhappiness, and crying was shown to the children. After a question was asked, the child pointed to the face that best expressed his/her feelings. For the more mature children, the five-point scales were explained and read out loud.

The length of the interviews depended on the child and ranged from approximately 15 to 90 minutes. The interviews were conducted over a four-month period each year.

Data Analysis

Data were entered onto a computer using the SPSS data analysis software system [SPSS 1993]. Analyses were performed using appropriate statistical tests for each item of the survey. The tests are described in the tables in the "Results" section of this article.

Reliability

Reliability was tested during the pilot study. The three kinds of reliability generally recognized for data collection instruments of these sorts are internal consistency, test-retest, and interrater [Winer 1971]. For this study the features of test-retest and interrater reliability were used. Not only had time passed between the two interviews (approximately four weeks), but a different interviewer was used. This means that the estimates of reliability derived from this study were conservative, that is, they were likely to be lower than either "pure" method. In this situation, it was not possible to conduct interviews by two different interviewers on the same day because of the burden to the respondent and concern for intrusiveness. The only available opportunity to test reliability with these interviewers and these children was to allow some time to pass between interviews. The test-retest study involved reinterviews by telephone of 44 respondents representing each interview category. The items selected for the study were "Yes/No" and five-point scale questions. Altogether, 60 items in the 11 interviews were asked twice.

The items selected for the reliability study were 12 "Yes/No" type responses and 44 five-point scale questions. These items were selected by the research team and the child welfare agency because they were believed to be those most important to the study objectives.

The "Yes/No" type responses were in perfect agreement, that is, they were the same 100% of the time. On the five-point scale questions, 49 out of 56 items were in agreement for an overall percent agreement rating of 87.5% [Wilson & Conroy 1993]. The instruments thus displayed acceptable reliability properties, as judged by the combination of test-retest and interrater criteria.

Validity

Validity in general concerns the degree to which a test measures what it is intended to measure [AERA et al. 1985]. In this study, face validity and content validity were informally established by utilization of a statewide advisory committee comprising experts in the field. Participants included statewide association representatives, advocates, service provider organizations, and the staff of the child welfare agency. The advisory committee reviewed and recommended revisions to the instruments.

Findings

Demographics

The children interviewed ranged in age from 5 to 18. At the time of their interviews, nearly all of the children were receiving regular dental and medical care and were in school or working on their GEDs. The majority of the children interviewed were living in family foster care in Cook County, the county in which Chicago is located.

The average time the children's cases were in the system reached a high in 1996 of 46.3 months. It had increased from 38.7 months in 1995, 42 months in 1994, and 43 months in 1993.

Overall Well-Being

The children were asked questions such as "Are you loved?" and "Are you safe?" The response choices to these questions were "always," "sometimes," and "never" and are outlined in table 1. Approximately four out of five of the children interviewed each year said they were "always" loved and "always" safe.

Differences Across Placement Type in 1995

Although data were stable across the four years, a pattern of differences across placement type was evident in the 1995 samples. When the data related to being loved and feeling safe were analyzed by placement type in 1995, children living in family foster care were more likely to say they were "loved" and "safe" as compared to their counterparts living in group care arrangements [Wilson & Conroy 1995].

Of the 100 children in kinship care interviewed in 1995, 94% said they were "always" loved and 92% of these same children were "always" safe. Children in nonrelative foster care ($N = 100$) said they were "always" loved 82% of the time. Of these same children, 92% said they "always" felt safe. By comparison, 46% of the children living in group care ($N = 100$) "always" felt loved and 64% of these same children said they were "always" safe.

TABLE 1
Children's Perception of Overall Well-Being, by Year

Year	Are You Loved? (% Always)	Are You Safe? (% Always)
1996*	82%	84%
1995*	86%	90%
1994	84%	87%
1993	87%	86%

* Indicates data were weighted [SPSS 1993].

The data indicate that children in kinship care are more likely to "always" feel loved than their peers living with nonrelatives in family foster care or their peers in group care. The most dramatic differences, however, are related to the comparison of children in family foster care with those in group care: the percentage of children in group care "always" feeling loved and safe was significantly lower. Treating the "do you feel loved" item as a three-point scale (1 = always, 2 = sometimes, 3 = never), the three groups' responses were subjected to analysis of variance. The group means were significantly different $(F = 2 8.84, df = 2, p <.0001)$. The least significant different posthoc test revealed that the mean for children in group care was significantly different from the two other groups. The mean for children in kinship care was 1.0505, for children in nonrelative foster care 1.2143, and for children in group care 1.7172. The children in group care were less likely than the children in family foster care to "always" feel loved.

Treating the "do you feel safe" item as a three-point scale (1 = always, 2 = sometimes, 3 = never), the three groups' responses were subjected to analysis of variance. The group means were significantly different $(F = 14.90, df = 2, p < .0001)$. The least significant different posthoc test revealed that the mean for children in group care was significantly different from the two other groups. The mean for children in kinship care was 1.0808, for children in nonrelative foster care 1.0900, and for children in group care 1.4000. Children in group care were less likely than their peers in family foster care to "always" feel safe.

Quality of Life

When asked if they were satisfied with their present living arrangements, the children's responses across the four years were highly consistent and positive: on average, more than four-fifths of the children (81.5%) said they were "happy" to "very happy" with their current living situations.

The results of the self-reported quality-of-life scale revealed significant increases in the children's satisfaction after placement. The children were asked to rate, on a 1 to 5 scale (with "5" the highest possible rating), 15 quality-of-life dimensions when they were living with their biological parents ("Then"). After they completed this evaluation, they were asked to rate the same items in out-of-home placement ("Now"). The quality-of-life dimensions were: health, how you look, school, playmates/friends, things you do for fun, clothes, comfort, food, place where you lived before/live now, your bedroom or private space, sleep, feeling loved, feeling safe, family relationships, and happiness. Table 2 shows the mean quality-of-life ratings. Internal consistency for the "quality-of-life scale" was examined via Cronbach's Alpha [Cronbach 1951]. Alpha for the 15-item "Then" scale was .93; alpha for the 15-item "Now" scale was .94. Alpha values above .80 are considered acceptable.

The means indicate the children reported that the quality of their lives was perceived to have improved by moving to out-of-home care.

Self-reported quality of life in 1995 varied across placement types. By combining the 15 quality-of-life items into a single scale, it was possible to test for group differences via analysis of variance. Children in group care gave significantly lower satisfaction ratings than children in kinship care and nonrelative foster care ($F = 2$ 6.63, $df = 2$, $p < .0001$).

TABLE 2
Children's Perception of Quality of Life, by Year*

Year	Mean "Then"	Mean "Now"
1996**	3.96	4.37‡
1995**	4.04	4.52‡
1994	3.71	4.48‡
1993	3.50	4.42‡

* Ratings were on a 1-5 scale, with "5" the highest possible rating.
** Indicates data were weighted [SPSS 1993].
‡ Indicates changes from "Then" to "Now" were significant by paired *t*-tests at the .01 level.

Perceptions of Child Welfare/Provider Agency

Three out of four children (76%) were "happy" to "very happy" with their caseworkers; interviewers also asked the children to explain their responses. The children's comments were transcribed verbatim and included in the reports. Most frequently, the children said their caseworkers were nice people, for example, characterizing the workers as "funny," "nice to talk to," and "easy to understand." Negative comments most often related to the caseworkers' inaccessibility, inability to visit often enough, and failure to carry out promises made. One child complained that her caseworker was not understanding, never visited or called, provided inaccurate information, and "even criticizes me."

When asked "Did you help your caseworker decide what was going to happen to you after you left your own family and were living somewhere else?," on average across the four years, fewer than a third (29%) of the responding children said "yes." If the child did not understand the terminology, the interviewers were instructed to use alternative terminology until they were convinced the child understood the question. One child commented, "It was like I wasn't even there." These data suggest that although children know what they want and can respond reliably, their input is not considered when the issue of permanency is debated.

When asked if there was anything they needed, approximately one-quarter of the children from 1993 to 1995 said "yes." In 1996, the percentage of children reporting they had unmet needs jumped to 47%. Without further research, it is difficult to ascertain the cause or causes of this dramatic increase.

Consistently, more than four out of five children who responded said DCFS or one of the agencies it contracted with to provide services "always" or "sometimes" helped. Despite the fact that the overwhelming majority of children believed these organizations had helped them, however, when asked to rate DCFS or the private agency, only 63% of the responding children rated these entities as "good" to "excellent" (see table 3).

Qualitative Data

The final section of the children's questionnaire asked several open-ended questions. One of these asked the children to tell the interviewers what they liked most about what had happened to them since they had left their parents' homes. The children frequently talked about being treated well, doing better in school, having friends, having improved self-esteem, being comfortable, having fun, having nice clothes, and having enough to eat. In response to what they liked least, they frequently talked about being separated from or not seeing their parents and siblings, losing their freedom, being teased or treated badly by other children, or not liking some physical aspect of where they lived (e.g., their bedrooms or neighborhoods).

Conclusion

Limitations

The limitations of the data reported herein must be made clear. First, the present report deals only with the responses of the children themselves. In each year of the annual client evaluation, foster parents and child care workers were also interviewed. During the first three years of the evaluation, biological parents were

TABLE 3
Children's Perception of DCFS/Private Agency

Year	Mean % Responding that DCFS/ Private Agency has "Always" or "Sometimes" Helped	Mean % Rating DCFS/ Private Agency as "Excellent/Good"
1996*	86%	65%
1995*	88%	63%
1994	82%	62%
1993	85%	60%

* Indicates data were weighted [SPSS 1993].

interviewed. Their responses are not reported here, but they were included in reports to the state child welfare agency [Wilson & Conroy 1993, 1994, 1995, 1996].

Second, there are several shortcomings in satisfaction research generally, such as respondents' desire to provide socially acceptable answers, memory difficulties, and response biases such as acquiescence and recency [Sigelman et al. 1981]. Although every effort was made to avoid these pitfalls in this body of work, these factors remain as threats to validity.

Another possible limitation is that the sampling strategies varied over the four years of research. Hence, pooling of the data must be done with caution, including appropriate weighting.

Finally, there may be some doubt about the validity of young children's answers in surveys of this kind. This study produced evidence that the children's responses tended to be stable over time and across interviewers. Future efforts to evaluate child welfare systems should include the voices of the children themselves, with all appropriate psychometric checks and cautions.

Interpretation of the Data

The Illinois Department of Children and Family Services (IDCFS) is one of the few child welfare agencies in the nation to ask service recipients to evaluate its performance. The outcomes documented herein, subject to the limitations noted above, offer policymakers and funders a unique opportunity to review current child welfare practices based on data gleaned from representative samples of children.

The data suggest that Illinois's out-of-home care system is received favorably by most of the children served, especially children living in family foster care. These findings can be used to assist decisionmakers in making purposeful plans for the future; developing new services and supports based on the children's input; targeting problems before they escalate; and redesigning, limiting, or discontinuing services that are not well rated.

For example, feeling "loved" and "safe" are key indicators of a child's well-being. When the data related to feeling loved and safe were analyzed by placement type in 1995, children living in family foster care were far more likely to "always" say they were loved and safe than were their counterparts living in group care arrangements. The 1995 analysis highlighted other significant differences in key indicators when family foster care was contrasted with group care: The children in family foster care consistently expressed greater satisfaction.

Kinship versus nonrelative foster care was examined in detail in the 1995 report. Few differences were found in the children's satisfaction among children in family foster care (kinship care and nonrelative care); large and significant differences, however, were found in the comparison of family foster care to group care.

Overall, the children's feedback reflects their satisfaction with out-of-home care, primarily family foster care. On average, the children were highly satisfied with their homes and their caseworkers, and their self-reported quality of life had improved in out-of-home care. The children also believed the child welfare agency or its contracted providers had helped them.

One of the deficits found in the child welfare system was the lack of input the children had in writing their permanency plans. Fewer than a third of the children, on average, helped their caseworkers to decide their permanency goals. The children also voiced complaints about the way they were treated by juvenile courts. Most frequently, the children said that no one listened to them in court or that the proceedings were so complex they didn't understand what was happening.

This research suggests two avenues for further investigation:

1. Why are children remaining in the system an average of nearly four years, while termination of parental rights occurs in fewer than 5% of the cases [Wilson & Conroy 1996]?

2. Why was there a marked increase in the number of children who said they had unmet needs in 1996 (47%)?

The data collected in these interviews provide a report card on children's well-being in out-of-home care, primarily family foster care, in one large child welfare system. The results were remarkably consistent from one year to the next. For the great majority of the children and from their own reports, the system is working. These findings are evidence that this child welfare system's emphasis on family foster care in placement decisions is producing positive outcomes for the children it serves.

The annual client evaluations summarized in this article are a reflection of the paradigm shift in all human services toward the measurement of recipients' satisfaction [Glosser & Wexler 1985; Conroy et al. 1987]. Kuhn [1963] showed how almost every significant breakthrough in the field of scientific endeavor begins with a break with tradition, with old ways of thinking, and with old paradigms. Evaluation of services by service recipients is a break with tradition, whether the recipients are children, persons with developmental disabilities, or those who are elderly. It is not a fleeting trend, but an essential tool that will be needed to lead decisionmaking on out-of-home care into the next century.◆

References

American Educational Research Association (AERA), American Psychological Association, & National Council on Measurement in Education. (1985). *Standards for educational and psychological testing.* Washington, DC: American Psychological Association.

Benedict, M. I., Zuravin, S., & Stallings, R .Y. (1996). Adult functioning of children who lived in kin versus nonrelative family foster homes. *Child Welfare, 75,* 529-549.

Child Welfare League of America. (1996). The odyssey is underway. *Children's Voice, 5* (4), 22.

Conroy, J., Walsh, R., & Feinstein, C. (1987). Consumer satisfaction: People with mental retardation moving from institutions to the community. In S. Breuning & R. Gable (Eds.), *Advances in mental retardation and developmental disabilities, 3* (pp. 135–150). Greenwich, CT: JAI Press.

Cronbach, L. J. (1951). Coefficient alpha and the internal structure of tests. *Psychometrika, 16,* 297–334.

Dubowitz, H. (1994). Kinship care: Suggestions for future research. *Child Welfare, 73,* 553–564.

Dunlap, K. (1997). Family empowerment: One outcome of cooperative preschool education. *Child Welfare, 76,* 501–518.

Gardner, H. (1996). The concept of family: Perceptions of children in foster care. *Child Welfare, 75,* 161–182.

Glosser, G., & Wexler, D. (1985). Participants' evaluation of educational/support groups for families of patients with Alzheimer's Disease and other dementias. *Gerontologist, 25,* 232–236.

Illinois Department of Children and Family Services (IDCFS). (1996). *Executive statistical summary.* Springfield, IL: Bureau of Quality Assurance.

Johnson, P. R., Yoken, C., & Voss, R. (1995). Family foster care placement: The child's perspective. *Child Welfare, 74,* 959–974.

Kuhn, T. (1963). *The structure of scientific revolution.* New York: Wiley.

Magura, S., & Moses, B. (1986). *Outcome measures for child welfare services.* Washington, DC: Child Welfare League of America, Inc.

Petit, M., & Curtis, P. (1997). *Child abuse and neglect: A look at the states—The 1997 CWLA stat book.* Washington, DC: Child Welfare League of America.

Risley–Curtiss, C. (1997). Sexual activity and contraceptive use among children entering out–of–home care. *Child Welfare, 76,* 475–499.

Sigelman, C. K., Budd, E. C., Winer, J. L., Shoenrock, C. J., & Martin, P. W. (1981). Evaluating alternative techniques of questioning mentally retarded persons. *American Journal of Mental Deficiency, 86,* 511–518.

SPSS, Inc. (1993). *SPSS base system syntax reference guide: Release 6.0.* Chicago: SPSS, Inc.

Wilson, L., & Conroy, J. (1993). *The final report of the 1993 annual client evaluation.* Tallahassee, FL: Wilson Resources, Inc.

Wilson, L., & Conroy, J. (1994). *The final report of the 1994 annual client evaluation.* Tallahassee, FL: Wilson Resources, Inc.

Wilson, L., & Conroy, J. (1995). *The final report of the 1995 annual client evaluation.* Tallahassee, FL: Wilson Resources, Inc.

Wilson, L., & Conroy, J. (1996). *The final report of the 1996 annual client evaluation.* Tallahassee, FL: Wilson Resources, Inc.

Winer, B.J. (1971). *Statistical principles in experimental design.* New York: McGraw-Hill.

Concurrent Planning:
4 Benefits and Pitfalls

Linda Katz

Concurrent planning—working with families toward reunification while developing alternative permanency plans—was designed to fit an out-of-home care population much like that projected for the year 2000 and beyond: very young, chronically neglected children from multiproblem families. As large-scale programs begin to develop nationally, those implementing concurrent planning must be aware of the pitfalls that can undercut its effectiveness, while keeping in mind the benefits it can bring by reducing the trauma experienced by children in placement.

Linda Katz, ACSW, is Training Coordinator and Adjunct Faculty, Northwest Institute for Children and Families, University of Washington School of Social Work, Seattle, WA.

Concurrent planning: To work towards family reunification while, at the same time, developing an alternative permanent plan. [Katz et al. 1994]

As the child welfare field prepares for the new millennium, it is timely to consider ways in which practice might be adapted to better serve children in placement in the future. Concern over the growing national foster care census and continuing dissatisfaction among social work professionals and government leaders with efforts to improve outcomes for children in care add further impetus to such efforts. Additional support is found in the Adoption and Safe Families Act of 1997 (ASFA) (P.L. 105–89), which reduces from 18 to 12 months the scheduling of the permanency hearing, defines parental conduct that obviates the need for reunification efforts, and cites concurrent planning as an appropriate practice. Concurrent planning, pioneered in Washington State in the early 1980s, was specifically designed for the population expected to be in out-of-home care after the year 2000: the very young child whose family's chronic pathology (often drug/alcohol related) has left the child drifting in out-of-home care [Katz & Robinson 1991]. The concurrent planning model addresses this difficult-to-treat family constellation by combining vigorous family outreach, expedited timelines, and potentially permanent family foster care placements to improve the odds of timely permanency for young children.

Roots of the Model

Between 1959 and 1979, a number of clinicians and researchers published seminal works on the existence of foster care drift and suggested solutions. Heymann and her colleagues in Chicago produced two reports that led directly to the present model, suggesting that an agency's focus on permanency *from intake* and a diagnostic use of parental visiting patterns could greatly reduce drift and facilitate earlier permanency [Epstein & Heymann 1967;

Chestang & Heymann 1973]. This clinical perspective fit well with the overwhelming statistical evidence showing the scope of foster care drift between 1950 and 1980, the extraordinary length of time needed to effect an adoption for a child in out-of-home care, the diminishing options for those children still in care after one year, the particularly slow process of case resolution for infants entering care, and the efficacy of court review in speeding case movement [Maas & Engler 1959; Festinger 1976; Fanshel 1978, 1979].

During this fertile period in child welfare's evolution, attachment theorists entered into the out-of-home care field, spotlighting the psychic damage caused by repeated placements, which were endemic to the system [Littner 1972; Bowlby 1979]. Their theories caused a tidal wave of controversy when presented as a basis for redesigning the way courts handle children's cases (e.g., the proposal that case movement be determined by "the child's sense of time," rather than adult and organizational considerations [Goldstein et al. 1973]).

In a related development, placement agencies began to report on their efforts to create a hybrid program, called foster/adoption, that would benefit children in care who were unlikely to return home [Gill 1975; Gill & Amadio 1983; Mica & Vosler 1990]. Although many positive outcomes were described, the concept had its critics, who were concerned with possible inherent ethical dilemmas [Lee & Hull 1983]. Nevertheless, the child welfare field continued to move in this direction of experimentation, in hopes of forging a case management method that would specifically speed planning for young children placed out of dire circumstances, and that would reduce moves and trauma.

The concurrent planning model of the 1990s is built on a foundation of 30 years of data on out-of-home care length of stay. It is informed by a large body of clinical insights on childhood attachment, and implemented through programmatic innovations tailored to meet the needs of children.

The Population

What will the out-of-home care population in the United States look like in the years beyond 2000? Using existing information, it is possible to construct a picture of the children child welfare will be serving and for whom policies and programs will need to be designed.

The number of children in out-of-home care has increased every year between 1983 and 1994, due to the failure of discharges to keep pace with admissions [Wulczyn et al. 1997]. Furthermore, there has been a "striking increase in the percentage of infants entering care... balanced by a noticeable decrease in the percentage of children entering care as adolescents" [Wulczyn et al. 1997: 16]. Wulczyn and colleagues also note that children who enter foster care under the age of one year have the longest length of stay of all age groups, and are disproportionately represented in the approximately 30% of children in care more than 30 months. This has come as a surprise to the child welfare field, which is accustomed to regarding infants in out-of-home care as less problematic than older, more disturbed children. "One way to quickly summarize this finding is that the foster care population can be conceptualized as two or more distinct subpopulations. One subgroup fits the permanency planning model and moves through the system fairly rapidly, with most exits resulting in reunifications. At the same time, other subgroups do not fit that model, and apparently stay in the system a long time" [Wulczyn et al. 1997: 64]. This latter subgroup comprises those who enter care under one year of age; its members tend to be disproportionately African American, American Indian, or Latino, and to come from families trapped in chronic poverty, substance abuse, and violence.

The out-of-home care population is made up predominately of children whose families live below the poverty line [Berrick et al. 1998]. Although physical and sexual abuse have been documented at high rates in poor families, the statistically clearest and strongest relationship is that between child neglect and poverty [Petit & Curtis 1997]. These authors show an increase in child poverty from 14% in 1969 to 21% in 1995, with the result that for American children under the age of 6, the present poverty rate is one in four [Petit & Curtis 1997: 195]. As poverty rates continue to rise, the child welfare field will need to prepare for an increase in child neglect.

To predict the future of out-of-home care, it is necessary to add to these data what is known about this country's present public policy. For example, what conclusions can be drawn from the decline in poverty among the elderly in our country (from 27% in 1966 to 12% in 1994), the same period of time that saw a dramatic acceleration in child poverty [Petit & Curtis 1997]? Clearly, national policy decisions about income distribution have proven to be detrimental to children. The movement away from public housing supports for poor families, the increase in food stamp and school lunch restrictions, the changes wrought by welfare reform, and the tightening of disability definitions under SSI contribute to this trend [Freundlich 1997; Lindsey 1997]. If there is no shift in the national policy climate, and if the connection between poverty and child neglect is accepted, then it seems reasonable to expect the child poverty rate to continue to grow, and with it, child neglect and maltreatment leading to out-of-home care. As ASFA indicates, concurrent planning will be needed to produce better outcomes for such a population.

A Lesson

Given the population in out-of-home care and its congruence with the concurrent planning model (designed for young children from chronically distressed families), there is a danger of expecting more than can reasonably be delivered. As with any paradigm addressing a complex social problem, overgeneralizations about what concurrent planning can do in treating society's symptoms should be avoided. Too often, promising new methods have been oversold, inaccurately predicting significant cost savings and reductions in placement rates. A useful history lesson results when one considers the fanfare that introduced intensive family preservation services (another innovation initiated in Washington State). The Homebuilders model, when reproduced on a large scale in states such as Michigan, Illinois, and California, was not able to show placement *prevention* at anything like the rate projected [Warsh et al. 1995; Wells & Tracy 1996]. Placements *were*, however, postponed, shortened, and made less restrictive (and thus less expensive). Evaluators, clinicians, and politicians sought to explain the "lack of success" of family preservation services. It was said the wrong families had been referred, the intensive services watered down, the clinicians poorly trained, the service not sufficiently standardized, or the wrong outcomes measured [Rossi et al. 1996].

In fact, family preservation is a necessary and useful element along the continuum of child welfare services. Programs are being developed all over the country that help prevent placement *for certain families* and reduce the extent of placement for others. These programs help fulfill the 1980 reasonable efforts mandate of P.L. 96-272, requiring the provision of preventive services before out-of-home placement whenever possible. In the haste to claim more than could actually be accomplished, disappointment was created where none was warranted.

Similarly, concurrent planning will not produce miracles. What it can legitimately claim to do is give case planning a clearer sense of direction and measurable goals. It has the potential to reduce the number of temporary placements children go through, to shorten the length of time in care overall by clarifying and respecting timelines, and to increase the candor and respect given to biological families and relatives by drawing them into case planning early. It can help keep out-of-home care temporary, as it was intended to be.

Evaluation Efforts

Attempts to build an evaluation component into concurrent planning programs are in an embryonic stage and existing outcome reports are scarce. Early published results showed the success of the original program (1981) at Lutheran Social Services (LSS) of Washington and Idaho at eliminating foster care drift for high-risk young children [Katz 1990]. At the time of that article's publication, the agency was showing an average length of care from intake to permanency resolution of 13.1 months, with 82% of the children having only one placement. All the children were placed in permanency planning family foster homes, and foster parent adoption was by far the most frequent outcome. By 1998, the program results had evolved somewhat: The length of care was even shorter, the rate of return home higher, and the placement disruption rate had declined [Spoonemore 1977].

A second published evaluation report describes the efforts of New York City's Children's Aid Society (CAS), which replicated the LSS model [Children's Aid Society 1993]. The children served were similar to those in the LSS program in age and family circumstances but unlike the LSS population, predominately African American and Latino. CAS's success in timely case resolution was notable: within 12 months, 25% of children returned home, 32% were adopted by foster parents, and 42% were placed with relatives.

Since both LSS and CAS are private nonprofit agencies with controlled caseloads, and both of their programs involved small numbers of children, the question of transferability to the public agency setting is critical. Recently, the public sector has begun to take on concurrent planning experimentation as well.

Three state agency concurrent planning efforts have produced unpublished preliminary reports. A one-year public agency project, modeled on Lutheran Social Services, operated in central Seattle from September 1988 through September 1989 [Robinson 1989], which coincided with the peak of Seattle's crack cocaine epidemic. Criteria for inclusion in the project mirrored those of the LSS program; the population served, however, was more heavily African American. The project began with the transferring in of 65 children with open cases. Within one year, 55 of those cases were completed (50 children had parental rights terminated for foster parent adoption or guardianship, four children returned home, and one child's placement converted to guardianship without a termination). At that point, funding for the project ended.

Sedgwick County, Kansas (Wichita), began a pilot "dual case planning" project in January 1996, using a privatized model with three nonprofit agencies contracting with the public agency to provide family support, permanency planning, and adoption services [Schmidt-Tieszen 1996]. The goal was reduced length of care and fewer placements, building conceptually on the LSS model. Cases chosen for the pilot generally met the LSS criteria. The only available report to date, produced eight months into the project, noted a slower than hoped for rate of placement of children due to a lack of sufficient permanency planning foster homes to receive them at the project's inception. Although nothing can yet be said about final resolution of the cases, no child has experienced more than one placement.

Combining new state-expedited permanency legislation with the concurrent planning method, Colorado is tracking its success county-by-county as it widens the scope of its implementation [Schene 1997]. Its first report compares two counties 18 months into the project, duplicating the LSS-recommended age of the children and their family circumstances and adding the research enhancement of control groups in each county. Early data show a high rate of achievement of early permanency in the experimental groups, a surprisingly high rate of family reunification, and a very low placement disruption rate.

Two sites beginning sizable three-year projects in 1998 have formal evaluation components. The Manchester (England) Adoption Society has begun a permanency partnership with several local authorities (public agency branches) built on the LSS model. At the same time, the Administrative Office of the Court in Frankfort, Kentucky, is implementing a concurrent planning project in three counties across the state through a federal Adoption Opportunities grant, also drawing on the LSS approach.

As programs are established, it will be important to provide for data collection on length of care, number of placement moves, percent of children returned home, and percent of adoption plans made voluntarily by biological parents, as well as the effects of ethnicity and geographic diversity on outcomes. Beyond immediate outcome data, follow-up studies on disruption rates in later years will be essential.

Implementing the Concurrent Planning Model

Components of the Model

While concurrent planning is a simple concept, its successful practice requires casework sophistication and attention to detail. It should be viewed as a *discipline* that takes into account every placed child's long-term prospects from the first day of placement [Ichikawa 1997]. To achieve the desired goals, *all* of the following must be reflected in practice.

Differential Diagnosis. Within the first 90 days of placement, the agency completes a standardized assessment of the family's likelihood of being reunited within the next two months, based on the family's history, relationship with the child, and demonstrated progress to date. Families with a poor prognosis are given a concurrent plan.

Full Disclosure. All families are given information about the detrimental effects of out-of-home care on children, the urgency of reunification, and the agency's concurrent plan to safeguard the child from drifting in care. The family's options are thoroughly and repeatedly reviewed with them, including the use of extended family resources and the option of voluntary relinquishment for adoption.

Timelines. The entire case plan is structured by the legal requirements for timely permanency. These timelines are explained to families as part of the "full disclosure."

Visiting. Vigorous efforts are made to institute frequent parental visiting, *even with ambivalent or unresponsive parents.* The agency's zeal in promoting visiting will result in either faster reunification or early decisionmaking in favor of an alternative permanent plan.

Plan A/Plan B. In every poor prognosis case, children are placed with a family willing and able to work cooperatively with the biological parents but also prepared to become the children's permanent family if needed. This could be a relative or a foster family. Such a placement is acknowledged openly to the parents and supported by the agency and the court.

Written Agreements. Parents are helped by workers to reduce the overall case plan to small steps, written down with or by them, on a weekly or monthly basis. This facilitates observable compliance and improvement, and provides documentation for the court of unsatisfactory progress if it should be needed.

Behavior (Not Promises). The agency and the court proceed based only on the progress (or lack of progress) documented by observations, service provider reports, and expert testimony.

Forensic Social Work. The agency provides its staff with ongoing legal training, consultation, and support, so that its social workers produce legally sound case plans, concise court reports, and competent testimony.

Success Redefined. The agency and the court define their primary goal as *timely permanency*, with family reunification as the first, but not only, option.

Common Initial Concerns

Agencies now beginning to integrate concurrent planning into their foster care programs often express at least three initial concerns: potential judicial disapproval, doubts that the appropriate children can be identified early, and fears that foster family recruitment will be unsuccessful. Based on the experiences of Washington state, these concerns should not be deterrents.

Judges' Views. While agencies certainly must develop their programs in collaboration with the courts, and educate their judges, judicial resistance has not been a major obstacle to concurrent planning. In fact, judges have been advocates for concurrent planning, even as they continue to hold agencies to a high standard for reasonable efforts.

Selection of Appropriate Children. Experienced workers and supervisors, using the "Strengths in Families" and "Poor Prognosis" assessment tools [Katz et al. 1994], have little difficulty identifying children unlikely to return home in the near future. Furthermore, these tools provide a uniform standard, substantiated in practice, for addressing legal concerns over the equitable application of prognostic assessments.

Recruitment of Foster Parents and Relatives to Take the Role of "Plan B." Recruitment of any kind of foster parents is a challenge, but not more so in concurrent planning. Agencies must prepare to educate the public on the concept and to offer enhanced training and support to caregivers. The foster parents' role is difficult, often painful, but families do come forward.

Pitfalls in Implementation

Experience in implementing concurrent planning has revealed a number of pitfalls to be avoided if programs are to be legally sound, honest, fair to all participants, and supported by effectively trained workers, relatives, and foster parents—the source of this model's success thus far. As programs move into large-scale implementation across the country, avoidance of these mistakes will be critical to their success.

Equating Concurrent Planning with Adoption and Minimizing Reunification Efforts. Child welfare's responsibility to provide services to parents must be fulfilled in good faith or we violate both ethical and legal standards. Concurrent planning is not mere window dressing for expedited adoption. If it becomes that, it will have sacrificed all integrity.

Failing to Accommodate Cultural Differences. In designing case plans, assessing attachment, and making service referrals, cultural differences must be acknowledged, not ignored. Failing to do so can set up minority families to lose their children. This fear has strong historical roots. Cultural competence is as necessary in concurrent planning as in any other instance of state intervention in families' lives.

Using Assessment Tools to Assess Child Safety, Rather Than the Potential for Foster Care Drift. Risk assessment models that measure the likelihood of physical harm or neglect are in wide use nationally to answer the specific question: Is placement necessary? [Fluke 1994]. Concurrent planning begins with placement, not with a determination as to whether placement will be necessary. Following placement, the early assessment phase clarifies a child's likelihood of leaving care quickly. The worksheets, "Strengths in Families" and "Poor Prognosis Indicators," do not assess child safety [Katz et al. 1994].

Assuming That Assessment Tools Will Infallibly Predict Case Outcomes. When a hypothesis is constructed that a particular child is at high risk for drifting in out-of-home care, it is a generalization of past experience over many cases; ultimately, however, it will be supported or proved wrong by the child's parents. Either way, through placement in a potentially permanent home, the child has stability while in care.

Investing in One Particular Outcome, Either Reunification or Not, Rather Than Allowing the Result to Evolve from the Family's Decisions and Actions. Cases sometimes stall because of a worker's (or a judge's) continuing wish for an outcome that seems remote. When early permanency is defined as the appropriate goal, the focus is kept on the child's situation.

Defining Staff as Primarily Enforcers, Rather Than Social Workers with Case Management Responsibilities. Goal-oriented case management is essential, but engaging parents in the process of decisionmaking for their family requires sound casework skills.

Designing Case Plans That Are Not Family Centered (i.e., the agency takes on responsibility the family should have). Parents have both rights and responsibilities. Concurrent planning supports their active role in visiting, engaging in services, and planning for their child's future.

Interpreting 12 Months as an Absolute Limit on Reunification, Regardless of Parental Progress. There is a fine line between the judicious use of time limits to prevent foster care drift, and a rote enforcement that ignores the full picture of parental motivation, effort, incremental progress, and a foreseeable reunification.

Alienating Community Treatment Providers by Not Collaborating with Them in Early Program Planning. Mental health and substance abuse treatment services have a different clientele than do child welfare services. Conflict over goals and timelines can arise unless all work to find common ground through joint staffings, multidisciplinary collaboration, family group conferencing, etc.

Expecting Workers to Implement Concurrent Plans Without Solid Legal Training and Ongoing Consultation. Efficacy in the legal arena is critical. Workers must be provided with the necessary knowledge and legal personnel to mold their case plans into workable legal plans.

Offering Foster Parents and Relatives an Estimate of "Legal Risk." When asking a family to promise stability to a baby or toddler, without knowing if that child will eventually return home, it must be made clear that the level of "risk" being taken is not quantifiable. There is no guarantee, except that the child will have the least detrimental experience in care possible.

Failing to Train and Support Relatives and Foster Parents. Caregivers taking on concurrent planning need specialized training to help them support the child's biological parents. Within the tenets of state confidentiality laws and policy, caregivers should be informed of the case plan. If the caregivers are not related to the child, they need to meet and get acquainted with the child's biological family. In all cases, they must support the treatment plan while the agency works toward reunification over a planned, limited period of time. Keeping the time period controlled makes this possible for caregivers. If the caregivers work against the parents, it is the agency's responsibility to intervene.

Benefits of Implementation

Clearly, the concurrent planning model is built upon an expectation of high-functioning foster families, social workers, and supervisors. To this end, training and workload levels must be congruent with these expectations. Application of the full model of concurrent planning as it was intended has the potential to yield a number of benefits for children and families [Katz 1990].

- The average number of placements per child will come down.
- The average length of stay in out-of-home care will come down.
- There will be more voluntary relinquishments, specifically for foster parent adoption and open adoption.
- Foster parents will keep in touch with a child returned to his or her biological parents, providing continuity of relationships.

- Biological parents who have previously relinquished a child will return with a later child, often seeking placement of the siblings together.

Converging Themes

As work in family foster care continues to evolve after the year 2000, common threads can be seen among the many programmatic innovations, including concurrent planning. For example, consider the assumptions underlying family-centered practice, family preservation services, family group conferencing, concurrent planning, and open adoption. All are strength-based and look for ways to support parents' abilities to solve problems and make decisions. All seek to diminish agency formality by providing services in the family's home, scheduling visits in the evenings and on weekends, and involving large groups of relatives in case planning. Confidentiality is deemphasized so that everyone involved in the child's life can contribute information and solutions. In addition, there is a growing comfort with close, personal communication between biological parents, relatives, and caregivers, and a willingness to assume the best about families meeting this challenge for the sake of the child's well-being. In these ways, knowledge about the nature of children's attachments and the importance of continuity in their lives is being operationalized in program design [Katz 1996].

A well-run concurrent planning program can minimize the enduring psychological harm caused to children by multiple placements and years in the limbo of out-of-home care. Although such efforts may not be a "miracle," they are an improvement that is sorely needed and worth our best efforts.◆

References

Berrick, J., Needell, B., Barth, R., & Jonson-Reid, M. (1998). *The tender years: Toward developmentally sensitive services for very young children*. New York: Oxford University Press.

Bowlby, J. (1979). *The making & breaking of affectional bonds*. London: Tavistock.

Chestang, L., & Heymann, I. (1973). Reducing the length of foster care. *Social Work, 18*, 88–92.

Children's Aid Society. (1993). *12 months to permanency*. New York: Author.

Epstein, L., & Heymann, I. (1967). Some decisive processes in adoption planning for older children. *Child Welfare, 46*, 5–46.

Fanshel, D. (1978). Children discharged from foster care in New York City: Where to-when-at what age? *Child Welfare, 57*, 467–483.

Fanshel, D. (1979). Preschoolers entering foster care in New York City: The need to stress plans for permanency. *Child Welfare, 58*, 67–81.

Festinger, T. (1976). The impact of the New York court review of children in foster care: A follow-up report. *Child Welfare, 55*, 515–544.

Fluke, J. (1994). An accommodation with risk. *Protecting Children 10*(4), 2.

Freundlich, M. (1997). The future of adoption for children in foster care: Demographics in a changing socio-political environment. *Journal of Children and Poverty, 3*, 33–61.

Gill, M. (1975). The foster care/adoptive family: Adoption for children not legally free. *Child Welfare, 54*, 712–720.

Gill, M. M., & Amadio, C. M. (1983). Social work and law in a foster care/adoption program. *Child Welfare, 62*, 455–467.

Goldstein, J., Freud, A., & Solnit, A. (1973). *Beyond the best interests of the child*. New York: McMillan Publishing Company.

Ichikawa, D. (1997). The Washington State Office of the Family and Children's Ombudsman. Personal communication.

Katz, L. (1990). Effective permanency planning for children in foster care. *Social Work, 35*, 220–226.

Katz, L. (1996). Permanency action through concurrent planning. *Adoption & Fostering, British Agencies for Adoption & Fostering, 20*(2), 8–13.

Katz, L., & Robinson, C. (1991). Foster care drift: A risk assessment matrix. *Child Welfare, 70*, 347–358.

Katz, L., Robinson, C., & Spoonemore, N. (1994). *Concurrent planning: From permanency planning to permanency action*. Seattle, WA: Lutheran Social Services of Washington and Idaho.

Lee, R. E., & Hull, R. K. (1983). Legal, casework, and ethical issues in "risk adoption." *Child Welfare, 62*, 450–454.

Lindsey, D. (1997). Changing our understanding of child welfare: Replacing the residual paradigm. *Journal of Children and Poverty, 2*(1), 5–30.

Littner, N. (1972). *Some traumatic effects of separation and placement.* New York: Child Welfare League of America, Inc.

Maas, H., & Engler, R. (1959). *Children in need of parents.* New York: Columbia University Press.

Mica, M. D., & Vosler, N. R. (1990). Foster-adoptive programs in public social service agencies: Toward flexible family resources. *Child Welfare, 69*, 433–446.

Petit, M. R., & Curtis, P. A. (1997). *Child abuse and neglect: A look at the states—The 1997 CWLA stat book.* Washington, DC: Child Welfare League of America.

Robinson, C. (1989). *Summary report on King High–Risk SEBES Project* (unpublished). Olympia, WA: Children's Administration, Department of Social and Health Services.

Rossi, P., Schuerman, J., & Budde, S. (1996). *Understanding child maltreatment decisions and those who make them.* Chicago: University of Chicago, The Chapin Hall Center for Children.

Schene, P. (1997). *Expedited permanency planning in Colorado.* Report prepared for the Colorado Department of Human Services (unpublished).

Schmidt-Tieszen, A. (1996). *Kansas Families for Kids annual progress report. Dual case planning: The Sedgwick County experience* (unpublished). N. Newton, KS: Bethel College.

Spoonemore, N. (1997). Program Manager, Lutheran Social Services of Washington and Idaho. Personal communication.

Warsh, R., Pine, B. A., & Maluccio, A. N. (1995). The meaning of family preservation: Shared mission, diverse methods. *Families in Society: The Journal of Contemporary Human Services, 76*, 625–626.

Wells, K., & Tracy, E. (1996). Reorienting intensive family preservation services in relation to public child welfare practice. *Child Welfare, 75*, 667–691.

Wulczyn, F. H., Harden, A. W., & George, R. M. (1997). *An update from the multistate foster care data archive: Foster care dynamics 1983–1994.* Chicago: University of Chicago, The Chapin Hall Center for Children.

Shared Family Care: Providing Services to Parents and Children Placed Together in Out-of-Home Care

5

Richard P. Barth and Amy Price

Shared family care involves the planned provision of out-of-home care to parents and their children so that the parent and the host caregivers simultaneously share the care of the children and work toward independent in-home care by the parent. This article describes several innovative types of shared family care arrangements that demonstrate promise in the protection of children and the promotion of family well-being. Emphasis is placed on the shared family foster care model, including its key elements, funding, and evaluation.

Richard P. Barth, Ph.D., is Frank A. Daniels Professor of Human Services, Jordan Institute for Families, School of Social Work, University of North Carolina, Chapel Hill, NC. Amy Price, M.P.A., is Senior Research Associate, National Abandoned Infants Assistance Resource Center, School of Social Welfare, University of California, Berkeley, CA. Support for this work was provided by grants from the Children's Bureau, Administration on Children and Families, U.S. Department of Health and Human Services, and from the Zellerbach Family Fund, to the National Abandoned Infants Assistance Resource Center.

Out-of-home care has evolved during the 20th century to stress closer work with biological families to encourage reunification [Pine et al. 1996], shortened time frames to reduce the length of separation between mother and child [P.L. 96-272; P.L. 105-89], and increased emphasis on concurrent planning (which calls for agencies to create back-up plans for children if reunification fails).

Although research has shown the difficulty of achieving and sustaining reunification of children with their biological parents [Berrick et al. 1998], in 1997, when permanency planning time frames were shortened by federal law from 18 months to 12 months [P.L. 105-89], proposals to increase resources for drug treatment and other support services were defeated in final bicameral negotiations. Whereas a significant portion of Title IV-B (Part II) funds must be used for family reunification services, no additional funds have been appropriated. The Title IV-E waiver experiments will provide some information about alternative ways to achieve reunification goals; many of these efforts, however, are focused toward kinship guardianship, and there are few concerted efforts to improve reunification. Child welfare enters the 21st century, then, with a clear vision about the appropriate timing and focus of child welfare services and with new legislation, but without new funding sources and in need of more ideas about how to accomplish its vision.

The slow rate of reunification from out-of-home care (approximately 20% of children younger than 6 will remain in out-of-home care for six years) and frequent reentry into care (approximately one in five children who go home return to care within three years) call for a more thorough understanding of what is likely to have gone wrong [Berrick et al. 1998]. Perhaps one factor contributing to this phenomenon is that when parents are separated from their children, they lack the opportunity to learn how to interact with them effectively and to deal with the frustrations that are a normal part of parenting. Additionally, during separation, parent and child miss the chance to adjust to the continual changes they experience as individuals and in relation to each other. Child abuse often occurs when there is stress on parents who themselves received deficient parenting and who experience isolation from their own families and other community supports [Gabinet 1983]. Having had limited role models for good parenting, many adults must learn for the first time how to be effective parents while struggling with their own recovery and/or other personal issues [Barth 1994; Finello 1995].

The passage of the Adoption and Safe Families Act of 1997 (P.L. 105-89), which encourages expedited permanency for children, gives parents even less time to prove their ability to adequately care for their children before losing their parental rights. To comply with this legislation without unnecessarily separating families, the child welfare system, along with communities and other public agencies, must offer parents the support and education they need to become adequate parents or to make the decision to relinquish their parental rights. *Shared family care* [Barth 1994; Price & Barth 1996] is one strategy that may be effective in helping families remain safely together or become permanently reunified in an expedient manner without harm to their children or without difficult separations. This article describes several shared family care models currently being used to support parents in the care of their children, and provides program descriptions and information to guide the expansion of shared family foster care as an important addition to current services.

Why Shared Family Care?

Shared family care (SFC) refers to the planned provision of out-of-home care to parent(s) and their children so that the parent(s) and host caregivers simultaneously share the care of the children and work toward independent in-home care by the parent(s). Shared family care combines the benefits of in-home services, which are not always enough for some families, with out-of-home child welfare services, which may be unnecessary to meet a family's needs or may be ineffective. It has been used to prevent the separation of parents from their children, and to reunify families by providing a safe environment in which to bring together families and children who have been separated. SFC may also promote more expedient decisionmaking by helping parents make the choice to terminate their parental rights; it provides stability for children while alternative permanency plans are being made.

Whereas traditional out-of-home care requires family separation and typically offers little support to assist parents in becoming better caregivers, SFC involves "reparenting," in which adults learn the parenting and living skills necessary to care for their children and maintain a household while concurrently dealing with their own personal issues and establishing positive connections with community resources. By providing a living laboratory in a safe, family environment, SFC can help families learn to make better decisions, to handle typical day-to-day stresses, and to live together as a family.

Parental involvement has long been viewed as critical to the successful return of a child to the family [Fanshel & Shinn 1978]. Efforts to involve parents in their children's lives through regular supervised visits and family support meetings, however, do not teach family members how to interact on a day-to-day basis. In contrast, SFC allows parents to receive feedback about their parenting styles and skills on a 24-hour basis and across many and diverse parenting tasks [Barth 1994]. It also provides an opportunity for evaluating a parent's skills through direct daily observation. Ultimately, by simultaneously ensuring children's safety and preserving a family's ability to live together, SFC may be effective at preventing unnecessary family separation, decreasing the number of children reentering the child welfare system, and expediting permanency for children.

Models of Shared Family Care

Various models of shared family care exist, some dating back to the middle ages [McCoin 1987]. Battered women's shelters have long provided shared care by arranging refuge for victimized families in private homes. The mental health community has been using private homes to provide family foster care to mentally ill adults since the late 19th century [Carling et al. 1987]. Family foster care for the elderly is also burgeoning [Mehrota 1991], and the practice of shared family care has a long history in many European countries.

In recent years, several types of shared family care living arrangements that keep parent and child together have emerged in the United States, including drug and alcohol treatment programs for adults that also offer treatment for children; drug treatment programs expressly designed for mothers and their children; and residential programs developed to offer care to pregnant and parenting mothers. A fourth model, child care homes, provides a residence and treatment for parents. Although this approach is common in Sweden and other European countries, to date, the authors know of only one such program in the United States.

Since 1979, Texas Baptist Children's Home (TBCH) has operated a 24-hour child care facility aimed at preventing the separation of mothers and their children who are at high risk of out-of-home placement [Gibson & Noble 1991]. Targeting families with very limited income and inadequate housing and parenting skills, the program includes family cottages, in which three to five single mothers live with their children for an average of four months [Nagle 1998]. One staff family also resides in each cottage to provide case management as well as role modeling and coaching in parenting, discipline, effective communication, meal preparation, daily planning, and other life skills. Group and individual counseling sessions are provided by a full-time therapist, and child day care is available while the parent is applying for employment, working, going to school, or attending appointments. Additionally, limited support services and financial assistance are available to families on an as-needed basis for one to two years after placement.

Because the mothers provide much of the child supervision,

the residential staff are not licensed care providers and the program is not eligible for federal foster care reimbursement. The mothers, however, continue to receive public assistance (TANF) while in placement as they work toward self-sufficiency. Between 1991 and 1997, the program served 185 families (496 individuals). Over 99% of those families successfully completed the program and remained intact upon graduation [Nagle 1998]. Of those completing the program in 1996, 92% were employed upon leaving, 4% were full-time students, and 4% were homemakers.

Slightly different from the TBCH program, shared family foster care uses community residents and one-to-one matching to offer care to parents and children together. This article focuses on the key elements of this emerging model, current efforts to provide shared family foster care in the United States, and lessons learned from these efforts.

Shared Family Foster Care

Shared family foster care refers to a situation in which an entire family is temporarily placed in the home of a host family trained to mentor and support the biological parents as they develop the skills and supports necessary to care for their children and live independently. Until recently, this model has been essentially unknown and unavailable in this country. In the past decade, however, several shared family foster care programs have emerged.

Shared Family Foster Care for Minor Mothers

Since 1989, the Adolescent Mothers' Resource Homes Project of the Children's Home and Aid Society of Illinois (CH&ASI) has been placing pregnant and parenting teens who are dependents of the child welfare system in the homes of "resource parents," who are typically (but not always) single women who have raised their own children [Children's Home and Aid Society of Illinois 1994]. The teen mothers assume full responsibility for the care of their children; the resource mothers offer the teens nurturance and support and assist them in developing the skills and finding the supportive resources they need for parenting. All resource families must participate in an eight-week preservice training as well as ongoing inservice training and support groups. They are licensed as specialized child family foster homes and compensated, through Title IV-E and state funds, at roughly twice the standard adolescent rate, but well below the group home rate (i.e., the per diem rate to the agency is $74.25, which is split evenly between the resource family—to cover basic needs of the client family—and administration) [Astone 1996]. Each teen parent must sign a contract, along with all members of the resource family, the CH&ASI social worker, and any other involved member of the teen's family, clarifying each party's responsibilities and commitment to the others [Children's Home and Aid Society of Illinois 1994]. The goal of the placement, which is intended to last an average of six to 18 months, is to prepare the mother to live with her child either at home with her family or independently, or to help the mother recognize if she is unable or unwilling to adequately care for her child and facilitate permanent plans for her and her child.

Similarly, the Children's Home Society of New Jersey's Extended Family Care (EFC) Program places teen parents with their children in therapeutic foster homes. Most of these teens were seriously neglected or abused (emotionally, physically, or sexually) during their own childhood and had no positive role models [Pressma & Stephan 1998]. The EFC program is designed to teach the teen mothers, through modeling and therapeutic intervention, how to appropriately care for their infants and themselves. The placements last from one month to three years, with 40% lasting at least one year, and 25% lasting at least two years. The annual cost of the program is approximately $28,721 for one mother and one child [Pressma & Stephan 1998]. These funds, provided through a contract with the state, cover a family's board and clothing as well as day care for the child while the teen mother attends school. Since its inception in 1984, EFC has served 250 mothers and their infants. Of those, approximately 85% have successfully completed the program and remained together [Pressma & Stephan 1998].

Shared Family Foster Care for Adult Parents and Their Children

In the past several years, two programs—Whole Family Placement Program and A New Life Program—have demonstrated that a shared family foster care model can also be used with adult parents and their children. Since 1990, Minnesota Human Service Associates (HSA), a treatment foster care agency in St. Paul, Minnesota, has sponsored placements of whole families with "host families" through its Whole Family Placement Program [Cornish 1992; Nelson 1992]. HSA began providing this service for homeless families with foundation funding. Presently, the Whole Family Placement Program serves families in a variety of situations, including parents reunifying with their children in out-of-home care, parents coming out of chemical dependency treatment or prison, parents with low I.Q.s, parents with mental illness, and parents leaving battering relationships [Cornish & Monn 1998]. Although most families consist of a single mother with one or more children, two-parent families and single fathers are also served through this program. Client families are typically referred by child protection and probation staff to prevent placement of children away from their parents, to reunite parents with their children who have been in out-of-home care, or to determine if termination of parental rights should be explored. Although participation in the program itself is voluntary, the children are often in the legal custody of the state.

One social worker works with approximately eight to nine families at a time, and participates, along with each client and host family, in developing a written contract outlining each party's responsibilities. Clients generally maintain primary responsibility for the care of their children, and the host families serve as advocates, resources, and mentors in parenting and daily living skills. Host families are licensed child family foster homes (with a case-by-case waiver from the state), and are reimbursed through federal Title IV-E* and general county funds at a per diem rate of $30 to $36.50 per individual in placement [Cornish & Monn 1998]. The host family's monthly stipend is expected to cover the client family's food and other basic living expenses while in placement. An additional $15 to $20 per person is billed to county social services for administration of the program.

Placements last from one month to two years, with an average duration of five months. Although the primary outcome objective is to keep families together while members work on identified problems and concerns and move toward "independent" living, the program also helps some families decide to terminate their parental rights and free their children for adoption. In these situations, the children can remain with the host family until a permanent arrangement is established. Since 1992, 110 families have participated in HSA's Whole Family Placement Program [Cornish & Monn 1998]. Of those, 53 parents moved with their children as a family unit on to independent living and ended involvement with child protective services; 24 parents placed their children for adoption; 19 parents left their children in care where they remained until alternative plans were made; and 14 families are still in placement. Of the 53 families who moved on to independent living, none of them had subsequent involvement with child protective services within six months after placement termination [Cornish & Monn 1998]. In contrast, approximately 12% of children who are reunified with their families after a regular nonrelative foster care placement in California reenter care within six months [Needell et al. 1995].

Since 1991, A New Life Program, at Crime Prevention Associates (CPA) in Philadelphia, Pennsylvania, has used a similar

---

* Minnesota ruled that Title IV-E foster care dollars can be used to reimburse the child portion of a whole family placement if the host family is a licensed foster care provider and the state has legal custody of the child. Other states may not allow such a broad interpretation.

model of shared family care as one component of its comprehensive service delivery system for African American women who are addicted to crack cocaine, are pregnant or have an infant, and have a history of out-of-home placement. For ten years, CPA has provided specialized family foster care for delinquent youths in "advocate" homes in the community as an alternative to institutional placements.

The primary goal of A New Life is to help women gain sobriety and maintain abstinence without losing custody of their newborn children. Along with providing substance abuse treatment and relapse prevention services, the program focuses on strengthening a woman's capacity to parent her child and to use community resources for assistance and support. To this end, many women are placed in mentor homes once they have demonstrated a capability and willingness to participate in the treatment program. Placements typically last three months and coincide with intensive, daily drug treatment and parenting skills training, with on-site child day care provided five days a week [Keyser & Beamer 1998]. During the placement, each mother maintains her role as primary caregiver of her newborn, and receives support and guidance from her mentor.

A New Life mentors are women from the community who share the same cultural background as the clients, and who are trained to support clients in their recovery, model good parenting behaviors, help assure clients' ongoing participation in the program, monitor client behavior, provide instruction in life skills, and provide clients and their children with a stable home from which to transition into independent living. In exchange, mentors receive $300 per week. These stipends were initially provided through a National Center on Child Abuse and Neglect (NCCAN) grant, and are currently funded through county departments of drug and alcohol abuse and child welfare.

Unlike HSA's program, clients retain their TANF and food stamp entitlements while in placement. A New Life places approximately 40% of each client's monthly TANF payment in a savings account for future housing, until the client completes the program. Clients must use the remaining amount, along with their food stamps, to pay for their own food and other personal needs. Upon completion of the mentor home placement, women move on to other transitional or permanent housing in the community. To address the lack of affordable housing in the community and the need for ongoing support, CPA renovated three homes to provide transitional housing for women with their children upon completion of their mentor placement. Women in these and other transitional living situations continue to receive training and support through A New Life and continue to work toward reunification with their older children in placement.

A 1995 study of the program indicated that women who successfully completed a mentor home placement were more likely than those who never entered a mentor home to complete the overall treatment program (33 weeks of treatment compared to 20 weeks) [Williams & Banyard 1995]. Follow-up interviews with clients revealed the importance of carefully screening mentors and making good personality matches between mentor and client, and of the mentors allowing clients to make decisions and respecting their decisions without judgment.

Current Efforts

In 1996, the National Abandoned Infants Assistance (AIA) Resource Center at the School of Social Welfare of the University of California at Berkeley used experience from these existing programs, and the ideas generated by a national Technical Expert Group of child welfare service providers and administrators, to produce *Shared Family Care Program Guidelines*. This publication provides information about SFC and guidance to agencies interested in using this model for families involved, or at risk of involvement, in the child welfare system. The AIA Resource Center helped establish two pilot projects in California and five in Colorado [Price & Barth 1997; Wahlgren 1997]. These demonstrations are intended to determine if shared family foster care can (and, indeed, should) become a viable alternative to traditional family foster care in the 21st century. To this end, the seven programs, which are administered through county child welfare agencies (several through contract with community-based organizations), are participating in an evaluation being conducted by the AIA Resource Center. The evaluation will follow participating families throughout their placements (approximately six to nine months) and for one year after placement to determine which families are most likely to benefit from a shared family placement and what benefits they receive. The evaluation will also consider the comparable costs of operating such programs; the characteristics of individuals who become successful mentors and their reasons for participating; recruitment, training, supervision, and support of mentors; and the types of services provided to participant families.

As the seven programs are at varying stages of development and implementation, it is too soon to report any findings at this time. Nevertheless, given the apparent success of HSA's Whole Family Placement Program and A New Life Program, and the national movement toward expedited permanency, time-limited placements of families, and flexible uses of funding, there is reason to expect and encourage an expanded use of shared family foster care in the 21st century. The passage of P.L. 105–89, which allows for child welfare waivers to ten new states each year, also provides an opportunity for states to use Title IV-E funds to pay for shared family foster care. The following information may be useful in facilitating the expansion of this approach.

Key Elements in Shared Family Foster Care

Although Shared Family Foster Care (SFFC) shows promise in protecting children and preserving families, it is not appropriate for everyone. Parents must demonstrate a real desire to care for their children and a readiness to participate in a plan to improve their parenting skills and life situation. Experience suggests that parents who are actively using drugs, involved in illegal activity, violent, or severely mentally ill (and not receiving appropriate treatment) are unlikely to benefit from this program. Parents in recovery, those with developmental disabilities, those who are socially isolated and those with poor parenting skills, are good candidates for SFFC.

Other factors influencing the effectiveness of the program are the quality of the mentors and the matching process. Although mentors must be knowledgeable about child development, child safety, and discipline, they must also have an interest and competency in working with adults, and an understanding of substance abuse, domestic violence, and developmental disabilities. Additionally, they must be willing to participate as a member of a multidisciplinary team, committed to helping families become self-sufficient, and able to work with cultural, ethnic, and stylistic differences among families, communities, and agencies. Therefore, careful screening, comprehensive training (initial and ongoing), and extensive support and supervision are critical to the success of a shared family foster care placement.

Equally important is the match between the participant family and the mentor. Both parties should have sufficient opportunity to meet each other before a placement is made. Typically, this should include at least one office meeting, one meeting in the mentor's home, and one trial overnight. Once a placement has been established, a "rights and responsibilities agreement" should be developed and signed by all members (age 12 or older) of the client and mentor families to clarify expectations of each. Given the importance of this process (which can take up to two weeks), SFFC cannot be used effectively in emergency situations. In some situations, parents may come to live with mentors before they are reunified with their children so that the mentor-parent relationship can be tested and strengthened.

The success of a placement also depends on the services and supports available to the family to help them develop the skills and resources they need for effective parenting and independent living. To this end, each participant family should have a support team that works with them to identify goals, develop an individualized family plan, and obtain necessary services to work toward the achievement of their goals. This team typically consists of the mentor, the child welfare worker, a family advocate or case manager, and anyone else involved with the family (e.g., mental health therapists, substance abuse counselors, child development specialists, probation officers).

Because SFFC programs serve intact families in private homes, state licensure of the homes is typically not required. Some programs, however, may choose to license mentor homes to enable a child to remain in that home with the same caregiver if the parent relinquishes her/his parental rights or is otherwise separated from the child. This alternative may require a waiver from the state licensing agency to allow an adult related to the child to reside in the same home; some states will not grant this. In any case, mentor homes should meet basic state health and safety regulations.

Financing Shared Family Foster Care

The monthly cost of SFFC is generally higher than that of basic family foster care, comparable to treatment foster care, and probably less than that of institutional care or intensive family preservation (see table 1). Because SFFC placements typically are shorter than traditional out-of-home care placements, however, SFFC appears to be, at a minimum, cost neutral. Factoring in the efficiency of placing more than one child in the same home with his or her parents, thereby eliminating the need for other shelter arrangements, SFFC may result in fiscal savings if it achieves permanency for children at an earlier point than traditional out-of-home care settings would.

State and federal family preservation programs are the most viable source of funds for shared family foster care placements,

TABLE 1

Estimated Cost of Caring for One Child/Family

Category of Care	Avg. Monthly Maintenance Cost	Med. Service Duration	Avg. Total Maintenance Cost
Intensive Family Preservation	$2,800[1]	1.5 months	$4,200
Basic Family Foster Care	$362[2]	14 months[3]	$5,068
Shared Family Foster Care[4]	*$1,575*	*5 months*	*$7,875*
Treatment Foster Care	$933[5]	14 months[3]	$13,062
Residential Group Care	$3,100[6]	13 months[3]	$46,800

1. Based on a family with one child. The average cost of services for a family with two children is estimated to be $3,400 [Yuan 1990].
2. Baker & Finchio 1995.
3. Based on California statewide averages [University of California at Berkeley].
4. Based on an average of the basic maintenance rate of A New Life program and Minnesota Human Service Associate's Whole Family Placement program (unpublished data).
5. Based on an average per diem maintenance rate of $31.10 per child [Knips 1998].
6. Based on an average daily maintenance rate of $75 to $250 [CWLA 1994].

case management, and mentor compensation. Title IV-E foster care and adoption funds can finance the placement of adolescent parents and their children in mentor homes; through federal waivers, Title IV-E funds can also be made available for the placement of adult-headed families in certain states. TANF funding also can be used to support participant families in SFFC and finance some of the support services. Other potential funding sources include state and local child welfare and substance abuse programs and programs for homeless families. Private resources can support planning, start-up, and evaluation, and help fill other funding gaps (e.g., respite, training, and aftercare).

Anticipated Outcomes and Future Implications

When parents are separated from their children, they develop other relationships, lifestyles, and interests. Some of those make it difficult for parents to rebuild their interest in resuming the care of their children and their capacity to parent. Shared family care works to ensure that parents and their children have adequate housing, a structured and safe environment, and models of successful living, and that children are protected. Not all parents will want this or be able to take advantage of it to renew their developmental growth. The willingness of a parent to try something with so many benefits, however, may be a signal of substantial readiness to fully engage in the struggle to be an involved parent. Indeed, some parents who have used their stay in shared family care for self-assessment have determined that they are not ready for the responsibilities of parenting, that they are comfortable with their child's living arrangement, and that they will relinquish their child for adoption.

It is too early to tell how SFFC will operate when it is more fully implemented. Also, given the limited information about outcomes for other programs in which mothers and children reside together, it is too early to tell which parents will do better in SFFC as compared to residential mother and child group homes or treatment. These are areas of understanding that will evolve during the coming decades.

Shared family care may be a model that operates best when combined with other approaches. For example, parent trainers skilled in social learning-based approaches to care have had a substantial and positive impact on parenting behavior [McMahon & Forehand 1984]. Although most mentors will have had positive experiences in parenting roles, not all will have mastered the skill of teaching ways of parenting. Yet, some of the gains from skilled parent trainers are lost or never realized because of the high stress environments in which abusive parents typically operate. Failures in using parenting skills may also result in lowered expectations and lowered likelihood of using those skills in the future, unless these negative evaluations are quickly countered [Bandura 1989]. Therefore, combining the relatively controlled and supportive environment that shared family care creates with powerful teaching tools may provide an optimal environment for change. It is just one of many possible ways of heightening the impact of shared family care to achieve successful reunifications from out-of-home care in a timely and cost-acceptable manner.

Conclusion

Although shared family care is a relatively new concept for child welfare services in the United States, it reflects age-old practices in the African American community, and is widely used in western Europe. Shared family care is one variant among many possible approaches to meeting the multiple needs of families who remain involved with and invested in raising their children but have had difficulty maintaining a lifestyle conducive to healthy child development. Although it shows promise toward keeping families together and facilitating expedited permanency for children, it is certainly not appropriate for all families and only one of many promising new approaches that blur the boundary between out-of-home placement and in-home services, including: (1) shared custody arrangements (e.g., joint guardianship and standby guardianship) for children of parents with AIDS; (2) matching community mentors to families to prevent family separation (e.g., HSA's Family Restoration Program, and the grandparent mentor programs emerging in Pennsylvania, Texas, and elsewhere); and (3) mentor/foster care arrangements for pregnant and parenting women in prison (e.g., Friends Outside's Las Comadres program in San Jose, California, where volunteers mentor pregnant women in prison and become foster parents to their infants until the mothers are released from prison). All of these options must be considered as the search continues for better and more efficient ways of protecting children and preserving families in the 21st century.

The fiscal mechanisms for paying for shared family care have arrived via waivers and the new expectations of the Adoption and Safe Families Act, which diverts significant portions of funds to family reunification. The Adoption and Safe Families Act requires the administration to prepare a report on performance-based incentive funding systems for Title IV-B and Title IV-E. Such a report could provide the impetus for the flexible funding that would allow the growth of shared family care. Conceptually, this is an idea that deserves attention and development. The strengths of the model, and experience with it to date, suggest that it should do well when compared to other, more fragmented ways of serving children and parents. By the 21st century, this model will have achieved enough maturity to be used in comparative tests against other approaches.◆

References

Aston, C. (1996). Supervisor, Independent Living Program, Children's Home and Aid Society of Illinois. Personal communication.

Baker, M., & Finchio, T. (1995). *APWA's 1994 survey of foster care maintenance rates.* Washington, DC: American Public Welfare Association.

Bandura, A. (1989). Human agency in social cognitive theory. *American Psychologist, 44,* 1175-1184.

Barth, R. P. (1994). Shared family care: Child protection and family preservation. *Social Work, 39,* 515–524.

Berrick, J. D., Needell, B., Barth, R. P., & Jonson-Reid, M. (1998). *The tender years: Toward developmentally sensitive child welfare services for very young children.* New York: Oxford University Press.

Carling, P. J., Levine, I. S., & Stockdill, J. W. (1987). Foster family care for people with long-term mental health problems: Report of a National Institute of Mental Health sponsored workshop. *Adult Foster Care Journal, 1,* 79–88.

Children's Home and Aid Society of Illinois. (1994). *Adolescent Mothers Resource Homes Project: Program Description.* Chicago: Author.

Child Welfare League of America. (1994). *Report to the U.S. House of Representatives Committee on Ways and Means.* Washington, DC: Author

Cornish, J. (1992). Fostering homeless children and their parents too: A unique approach to transitional housing for homeless families. *Community Alternatives: International Journal of Family Care, 4,* 44–59.

Cornish, J., & Monn, S. (1998). *Shared family care for families in child protection and child welfare.* Presentation at Families Helping Families Conference, February 19, 1998, San Francisco, CA.

Fanshel, D., & Shinn, E. (1978). *Children in foster care: A longitudinal investigation.* New York: Columbia University Press.

Finello, K. M. (1995). Family reunification: Ready or not, here I come. *The Source, 5*(1), 8–10.

Gabinet, L. (1983). Shared parenting: A new paradigm for the treatment of child abuse. *Child Abuse and Neglect, 7,* 403–411.

Gibson, D., & Noble, D. N. (1991). Creative permanency planning: Residential services for families. *Child Welfare, 70,* 371–382.

Keyser, J., & Beamer, D. (1998). *Shared family care for drug addicted women and their infants.* Presentation at Families Helping Families Conference, February 19, 1998, San Francisco, CA.

Knips, C. (1998). Business Administrator, Professional Association of Treatment Homes. Personal communication.

McCoin, J. M. (1987). Adult foster care: Old wine in a new glass. *Adult Foster Care Journal, 1*(1), 21–41.

McMahon, R. J., & Forehand, R. (1984). Parent training for the noncompliant child: Treatment outcomes, generalization, and adjunctive therapy procedures. In R. Dangel & R. Polster (Eds.), *Parent training: Foundation of research and practice* (pp. 298–328). New York: Guilford.

Mehrota, C. M. (1991). Foster care for older adults: Issues and evaluations. *Home Health Care Services Quarterly, 12,* 115–136.

Nagle, D. (1998). Texas Baptist Children's Home, Roundrock, TX. Personal communication.

Needell, B., Webster, D., Barth, R. P., & Armijo, M. (1995). *Performance indicators for child welfare services in California: 1995.* Berkeley, CA: Child Welfare Research Center, School of Social Welfare, University of California.

Nelson, K. M. (1992). Fostering homeless children and their parents too: The emergence of whole-family foster care. *Child Welfare, 71,* 575–584.

Pine, B., Krieger, R., & Maluccio, A. (1996). *Together again: Family reunification in foster care.* Washington, DC: Child Welfare League of America.

Pressma, D., & Stephan, C. (1998). *Extended family care for teen mothers.* Presentation at Families Helping Families Conference, February 19, 1998, San Francisco, CA.

Price, A., & Barth, R. P. (1996). *Shared family care program guidelines.* Berkeley, CA: Abandoned Infants Assistance Resource Center, School of Social Welfare, University of California at Berkeley.

Price, A., & Barth, R.P. (1997). Shared family care: Child protection without parent-child separation. *Protecting Children, 13*(3), 15–16.

University of California at Berkeley Foster Care Database (unpublished data).

Wahlgren, C. (1997). National dateline: Colorado. *Protecting Children, 13*(3), 23.

Williams, L. M., & Banyard, V. L. (1995). *A New Life: An evaluation of a family reunification and child abuse prevention program for crack-addicted women and their children.* Philadelphia: Crime Prevention Association of Pennsylvania.

Yuan, Y-Y. (1990). Cost analysis. In Y-Y. T. Yuan & M. Rivest (Eds.), *Preserving families: Evaluation resources for practitioners and policymakers.* Newbury Park, CA: Sage Publications.

Professional Foster Care:
6 A Future Worth Pursuing?

Mark F. Testa and Nancy Rolock

This article reports on a study comparing the performance of a professional foster care program and two specialized programs in Cook County, Illinois, with random samples of kinship and nonrelative family foster homes. Professional and kinship foster care consistently outperformed the specialized programs and the nonrelative care in terms of stability, sibling placement, restrictiveness of care, and proximity to the child's community of origin. While the former two program types also do slightly better than the latter in achieving permanent living situations, the professional foster care program had difficulty moving children to adoptive homes or subsidized guardianship. Implications of these differences for the evolution of family foster care in the next century are considered.

Mark F. Testa, Ph.D., is Associate Professor, and Nancy Rolock, M.A., is Project Director, School of Social Service Administration, University of Chicago, Chicago, IL.

The professionalization of foster parenting is the latest trend in the evolution of family foster care. As more women enter the paid labor force, child-placing agencies are facing new difficulties in recruiting sufficient numbers of families willing to volunteer to become foster parents [Kahn & Kammerman 1990; U.S. General Accounting Office 1989]. The shortage is especially acute in central-city neighborhoods where the loss of a stable employment base and the declining presence of two-parent families have sharply reduced the supply of adults who can afford to care voluntarily for foster children at the prevailing boarding rates offered by public and private agencies [Chamberlain et al. 1992]. Consequently, most family foster home vacancies are located in suburban communities far away from the central-city neighborhoods where the families of a majority of children in out-of-home care reside.

The shortage of voluntary family foster homes and the spatial mismatch between placement needs and foster home supply are trends that are likely to intensify in the next century. Public policy appears to be evolving in two different directions to deal with these developments. The first consists of tapping into the natural altruism of kin to look after related children by adapting licensing standards and boarding rates to the particular circumstances of extended family care. Since the mid-1980s, kinship foster care has been the fastest growing component of formal foster care in the United States [Testa et al. 1996]. The second direction being taken involves paying foster parents for their labor, either indirectly by placing children in need of specialized foster care with them, or directly by hiring them as paid professional staff. *Specialized foster care* is the care of children with behavioral, developmental, emotional, or medical needs above and beyond those of average children in out-of-home care. Specialized foster caregivers typically receive a monthly board payment that is larger than that received by foster parents caring for children who do not fall into a special-needs category. *Professional foster care*, in the context of this paper, involves trained, professional foster parents who are paid an annual salary for foster parenting above and beyond any board payments made by the state on behalf of the children; most of them care for children with special needs. The movement toward specialized and professional foster care has been accelerating since the early 1990s [Barth et al. 1994].

Both strategies for dealing with the dual problems of foster home shortage and the spatial mismatch between need and supply are bringing to the surface long-standing controversies over the appropriate balance between family altruism and monetary incentives as motives for becoming foster parents [Zelizer 1985]. On the one hand, critics of kinship foster care are raising warning flags about kinship care's subverting the aims of welfare reform by becoming an "Aid to Relatives with Dependent Children" program [Charen 1997]. On the other hand, critics of professional foster care are voicing concerns about robbing family foster care of the essential qualities of family life—informality, spontaneity, and unconditionality [Lemay 1991]. These concerns are likely to increase in salience in the coming century, especially if kinship and professional foster care continue to displace traditional, voluntary family foster care as the dominant mode of out-of-home care.

This article takes stock of recent developments in the evolving organization of family foster care. In the study reported here, public administrative data collected on a professional foster care program and two specialized foster home recruitment programs in Cook County, Illinois, are compared with random samples of kinship and regular foster homes. The dimensions of comparison derive from the guiding principles of child welfare intervention, which emphasize:

- *Community-based care*—children should be looked after in family foster homes nearest to their community of origin;
- *Family integrity*—sibling groups should be cared for together in the same family foster home;
- *Continuity of care*—children should be maintained continuously in the same family foster home;

- *Least restrictive care*—children should be looked after in the least restrictive setting; and
- *Permanency*—children should be reunified with their biological parents as soon as safety is assured or else should be placed in alternative permanent homes.

To justify paying a salary to foster parents, agencies must demonstrate that professional foster care is able to achieve these goals more efficiently and effectively than would reliance on traditional, voluntary foster parent recruitment. By assessing how specialized and professional foster care compare with kinship and nonrelative family foster care, additional insight can be obtained on the extent to which professional foster care is a future worth pursuing.

Background

As with earlier changes in family foster care, the movement toward specialized and professional forms of care parallels changes in other spheres of domestic life. Historically, family foster care has patterned itself after the prevailing mode of household organization in society. When apprenticeship was a common feature of domestic life in the 18th century, many dependent and neglected children were bound out to families who provided care and tutelage in exchange for the children's labor [Breckinridge 1939]. With the demise of apprenticeship after the Civil War, child-placing agencies started to reimburse foster families for looking after dependent and neglected children by offering monthly boarding stipends [Hasci 1996]. These amounts were kept modest because farm families could still benefit from the child's labor. It was also thought that family altruism should be the primary motive for becoming a foster parent [Zelizer 1985].

As child labor laws in the first part of the 20th century began to confine children's "workplace" to the schools, child-placing agencies responded by emphasizing the voluntaristic aspects of foster parenting and targeting their recruitment accordingly.

Monthly boarding stipends were supplemented with county and state funds, and family foster homes were screened (later licensed) to ensure that funds went toward meeting the needs of public wards in private family care.

Public and private reliance on licensed boarding care was able to keep up with placement demand reasonably well until the 1970s, when women began to enter the paid work force in record numbers. As more and more women substituted paid employment in the labor market for unpaid labor in the home, the supply of voluntary family foster homes dwindled. The shortage reached a crisis of sorts in the mid-1980s as the number of children in out-of-home care began to rise, from 280,000 in 1986 to 400,000 in 1990 [Tatara 1998]. The current population of children in out-of-home care is estimated at more than 500,000 [Tatara 1998]. Public and private agencies were able to offset the loss of traditional voluntary homes by developing special approval and payment standards for the recruitment of relatives as foster parents. In addition, they developed specialized foster care programs that provided a higher boarding stipend to nonrelated families who agreed to look after children with special behavioral, developmental, emotional, or medical needs.

The professionalization of the role of foster parent pushes the trend of compensating foster parents for their labor to its logical conclusion. By hiring foster parents as paid employees, agencies are in a better position to deal with the dual problems of foster home undersupply and spatial mismatch between child need and home availability. Offering annual salaries in the $15,000 to $25,000 range in addition to foster care boarding stipends helps to remove one of the major obstacles to foster-home recruitment in central-city neighborhoods: the limited financial means of many local residents. In 1986, the Salvation Army Social Service for Children in New York addressed the shortage of foster parents by paying foster parents to recruit new foster parents. They found that with adequate support systems and training, paid foster parents are very good recruiters: they increased the agency's foster care capacity by 49% [Smith & Gutheil 1988]. By including foster parents as paid members of a professional team, agencies are also able to legitimate the increasingly complex demands that are being placed on foster parents. These include both the specialized care of special-needs children and the skillful balancing of the multiple and competing goals of child welfare intervention in regards to family preservation, child safety, and concurrent permanency planning. Meyer [1985] contended that hiring foster parents as professional staff with "real wages, personnel practices, training expectations, and rewards" will produce foster caregivers who are better prepared to deal with the unique problems of the children placed in their care. Finally, by paying foster caregivers, agencies are able to acknowledge the work value of foster care in the dominant medium of exchange in contemporary society—cash income.

Study Design

This study grew out of an evaluation of a professional foster care program in Chicago, Illinois, that the authors conducted in the spring of 1996 [Testa et al. 1998]. The full evaluation, which was commissioned and paid for by the sponsoring agency, included a comparative analysis of available state administrative data on the program and three comparison groups: a random sample of regular family foster homes and two similar family foster care recruitment programs in Cook County, Illinois.

This study updates the original evaluation with more recent administrative data. It also replaces the original random sample of regular family foster homes in Cook County, Illinois with random samples of kinship and nonrelative family foster care homes. The random samples are restricted to homes that received children during the original period of observation: December 1, 1994, to September 30, 1996. The placement and permanency experiences of children are tracked with an additional year's worth of administrative data through September 30, 1997. None of these programs are considered specialized family foster care programs. Brief descriptions of the programs follow.

Professional Foster Care (PFC) Program

The PFC program began in 1994 under a grant from the Illinois Department of Children and Family Services (IDCFS). Children are considered appropriate for the program if they are to be placed together in sibling groups of three or more and at least one of the children exhibits special developmental, behavioral, emotional, or medical needs. Foster parents are paid an average salary of $16,000 as well as $600 per child in monthly board payments.

Urban Foster Care (UFC) Program

The UFC program was initiated by IDCFS in 1994 to expand foster home recruitment in Chicago's least-served neighborhoods. In lieu of paying caregivers a salary, the UFC program provides them with a tax-free housing subsidy and security deposit (up to $550 per month), as well as an average monthly board payment of $350 per child.

Sibling Foster Care (SFC) Program

The SFC program was started by IDCFS at the same time as the UFC program. Its recruitment goals are similar to those of the UFC program. In addition, it focuses on finding homes for sibling groups of two or more. The SFC program offers caregivers a tax-free housing subsidy and security deposit that are slightly higher than those of the UFC program (up to $800 per month), in addition to an average monthly boarding payment of $350 per child.

Regular Foster Care (RFC) Program

IDCFS places children in licensed family foster homes that either it or private child welfare agencies supervise. Most foster families receive regular boarding payments at the average monthly amount of $350 per child as reimbursement for the cost of care.

Home of Relative (HMR) Program

In July 1995, IDCFS implemented a two-tier system of home certification and payment for relative foster parents. Prior to this, IDCFS extended full monthly board payments averaging $350 per child to all relative caregivers regardless of their licensing status. Under the two-tier system, the full board payment is now reserved for kinship homes that satisfy the same licensing standards that apply to nonrelated homes. Extended families who are not licensed, but who pass a basic home safety and criminal background check, receive a monthly stipend equal to the AFDC standard of need of $252 per child. Because the two-tier system was introduced during the period of observation, some of the kinship homes in the HMR random sample operated under the old rules, some under the new rules, and most under both.

Findings

Table 1 presents the results on the comparative performance of the five program types.*

Community-Based

Both the PFC and UFC programs do significantly better than regular family foster care programs in placing children nearest to the neighborhoods of their biological parents. Neither, however, matches the close distances that are achieved by placement in kinship homes. Approximately one-third of the children in kinship care homes reside two miles or less from where their parents reside. As the distances from the home community exceed

---

* The UFC, SFC, and PFC program statistics are based on complete census counts. Therefore, there is no sampling error for these estimates. The HMR and RFC program statistics are based on random samples of homes. HMR and RFC estimates between 20% and 80% have a 95% confidence interval of ±3%; estimates between 10% and 20% have a 95% confidence interval of ±2%. With the exception of the statistics on least restrictive care, all of the remaining percentage differences between the census counts and the sample estimates are statistically significant at the .05 level.

TABLE 1

Foster Care Performance Indicators for Children in Family Foster Care by Type of Care

Performance Indicators	HMR[1]	RFC[2]	Type of Care UFC[3]	SFC[4]	PFC[5]
1. Community-Based Care: How far away do children live from the homes of their biological parents (cumulative distance)?					
≤2 miles	34.6%	7.0%	16.7%	9.5%	3.2%
≤5 miles	66.6%	26.2%	44.5%	31.9%	43.7%
≤10 miles	74.5%	52.4%	73.3%	66.8%	84.9%
≤15 miles	85.6%	71.3%	94.1%	85.2%	96.8%
2. Family Integrity: What percentage of siblings live in the same home?					
Sibling group of 3	56.0%	24.0%	18.8%	60.0%	75.0%
Sibling group of 4	46.6%	12.9%	8.0%	8.5%	70.0%
Sibling group of 5	34.4%	3.1%	11.6%	10.9%	37.0%
3. Continuity of Care: What percentage remained in the same home as of 9/30/97?					
In same home	46.8%	20.2%	40.4%	36.0%	57.2%
Move to another	30.8%	59.6%	50.3%	51.7%	25.8%
4. Least Restrictive Care: What percentage moved to residential or group care?					
Moved to residential/group	5.1%	6.0%	3.2%	5.3%	3.1%
5. Permanency: What percentage attained permanency as of 9/30/97?					
Returned home	7.4%	7.1%	4.8%	5.3%	13.2%
Adopted	5.4%	4.7%	0.3%	0.6%	0.0%
Subsidized guardianship	1.5%	0.1%	0.0%	0.0%	0.0%

1. Home of Relative: N = 995 homes; 2,159 children.

2. Regular Foster Care: N = 852 homes; 3,167 children.

3. Urban Foster Care: N = 124 homes; 315 children.

4. Sibling Foster Care: N = 78 homes; 362 children.

5. Professional Foster Care: N = 33 homes; 159 children.

10 miles, the advantage shifts to the PFC and UFC programs. At these ranges, however, kinship placement probably confers greater advantages than shorter travel distances between the foster home and the parental home. The same cannot be said for children in nonrelative family foster care. A little under one-half (47.6%) of children in nonrelative family foster care are placed 10

miles or more from their parental homes and 28% are located 15 miles or more away from their communities of origin.

Family Integrity

Whenever children cannot be safely maintained with their parents, good practice suggests that family integrity should be upheld by placing sibling groups together in the same home [Ward 1984]. This principle, however, has been difficult to realize through regular family foster care, especially for large sibling groups. As table 1 shows, less than one-fourth (24%) of the children in sibling groups of three are able to remain together in regular foster care. Even the UFC program underperforms on this measure. On the other hand, sibling groups are more likely to remain intact in kinship care. A little over one-half (56%) of sibling groups of three in the HMR sample are able to stay together when placed in a relative's home. Equally encouraging are the high rates of intactness that are achieved by programs purposively designed for sibling care. Both the SFC and PFC programs are able to care for most sibling groups of three in the same home. Oddly, this comparative advantage disappears in the SFC program for sibling groups of four. Meanwhile, the PFC program is able to sustain the advantage: 70% of sibling groups of four are able to stay together in the same home. When the sibling group size exceeds four, however, the performance of the PFC program starts to flag.

Continuity of Care

Too often the trauma children experience at their separation from their biological parents is compounded by their repeated movement while in care from home to home. Thus, it is disconcerting to find that only one out of five children (20.2%) who were in regular foster care between December 1994 and September 1996 were still in the same foster home as of September 1997 (see table 1). Most of the children (59.6%) had changed homes at least once. Even though children in the UFC and SFC programs were more likely to stay in the same home than children in regular family foster care, they didn't fare much better on placement stability: 50.3% and 51.7%, respectively, changed homes. It is only when children were placed in the PFC or HMR programs that a modest level of placement stability was secured: 46.8% of children in HMR care and 57.2% of children in PFC remained in the same home. Still, the fact that 26% to 30% of children in these programs did change homes at least once raises the questions of how truly stable even HMR and PFC homes are.

Least Restrictive Care

One of the justifications provided for PFC programs is that it is less costly to pay foster parents an annual salary than it is to maintain a child in residential or group care. The logic of this economic comparison, however, assumes that the children would otherwise have ended up in residential or group care were it not for placement in the PFC program. Although it is impossible to estimate the latent risk of children entering residential care from the PFC program in the absence of random assignment, simple comparisons among the five program types suggest that the underlying probability is low: 6% of those in the RFC sample moved to residential or group care during the observation period. Even though the comparable risk in the PFC program is only one-half as large, the true underlying propensity toward institutionalization would have to be much higher before the differential cost of PFC as compared to residential care ($100 vs. $250 per day) could yield offsetting savings. Nonetheless, children in the PFC program face lesser risks of being "stepped-up" to more restrictive levels of care than children in most other types of care.

Permanency

The definitive indicator of successful child welfare intervention is whether children can be safely restored to the custody of their parents or placed into an alternative permanent home if reunification proves unattainable. By this measure, the comparative advantage is with kinship foster care, which registered a combined permanency rate of 14.3% during the period of observation, although it is extremely doubtful that such a result would have been obtained several years ago when the conventional wisdom was that relatives don't adopt [Thorton 1991]. More recent research, however, shows that when certain myths are dispelled and the legal and financial advantages are fully explained, much greater proportions of extended kin are willing to consider adoption than practitioners have previously supposed [Testa et al. 1996]. IDCFS has been able to act on these insights and greatly increase the rate of kinship adoptions. In addition, Illinois became the second state in the nation (after Delaware) to receive a federal waiver in 1996 that authorized the claiming of federal Title IV-E reimbursements for subsidies paid to relative caregivers and foster parents who assume private guardianship responsibilities for state wards. Although still in the formative stages of implementation, it is the availability of subsidized guardianship that boosts the permanency ranking of kinship care above regular family foster care.

Were it not for its complete lack of adoptions or guardianships, the PFC program would have easily outperformed the other programs with regard to permanency. The PFC program's reunification rates are almost twice as large as those of the HMR and RFC programs. But it is precisely this deficiency in securing alternative permanent homes for children in the PFC program, as well as in the UFC and SFC programs, that raises troubling doubts about whether the professionalization of foster care is indeed a future worth pursuing.

Discussion

The results of this comparative analysis form a consistent pattern. If the types of care are arrayed along a continuum from family altruism to full monetary compensation, performance levels follow a curvilinear shape. That is, the two ends of the continuum, kinship foster care and professional foster care, rank highest on the performance scales, while the middle of the continuum (i.e., regular family foster care) ranks consistently lower.

One way of interpreting this pattern is to equate family foster care performance with the willingness of foster parents to invest themselves in the care of other people's children. This willingness, in turn, is a function of the degree of altruism that foster parents bring to the task and the amount of monetary compensation they receive in exchange. Both sorts of incentives are substitutable within limits, so that similar levels of family foster care investment can be achieved either by offering greater monetary compensation or by tapping into larger reservoirs of altruism. Because levels of altruism increase the more closely related the caregivers are to the children [Hamilton 1964], public child welfare systems have been able to recruit additional family foster homes without raising foster care boarding rates by incorporating extended families into the formal out-of-home care system. Likewise, they have been able to augment the supply of family foster homes by providing higher compensation to nonrelatives through specialized and professional foster care programs.

As the results demonstrate, similar levels of performance can be attained either by providing foster parents with additional compensation (as in the case of professional foster care) or by recruiting foster parents with greater levels of altruism (as in the case of kinship foster care). How far in either direction public child welfare systems will be willing to move in the next century is an issue that undoubtedly will garner much attention.

Recent trends in the use of kinship foster care suggest that public child welfare systems will continue to explore ways of exploiting the altruistic impulses of kin to look after their own. To do so effectively will likely require the development of special home certification and payment procedures for kinship homes that do not offend constitutional principles of equal protection or create perverse incentives for informal family caregivers to enter the formal family foster care system, as happened in Illinois prior to the 1995 reforms [Testa et al. 1996]. Even if state legislatures and the U.S. Congress were to statutorily carve out kinship foster care as a separate component of formal out-of-home care, however, there would still be hundreds of thousands of children who would require placement in nonrelative foster homes.

The professionalization of family foster care offers a means of approximating the high performance levels of kinship care for children who lack family members willing to assume the responsibility of care. There are important limits, however, on the substitutability of paid employment for family altruism that point to future problems if professionalization were ever to displace voluntary foster caregiving.

One major child welfare dilemma that is accentuated by the trend toward the professionalization of family foster care is the question of what should be done with the children who cannot be reunited with their parents. Indicative of these potential problems is the poor performance of the PFC, UFC, and SFC programs with respect to adoption and guardianship (see table 1).

The authors' original evaluation found that about one-third of the children in the PFC program had a permanency goal of adoption or long-term foster care. The foster parents said they would consider adopting in only one-third (32%) of these cases. Foster parents ruled out adoption in 41% of the cases, and the remaining 27% fell into the "don't know" category. The survey of professional foster parents revealed that some of the obstacles to converting foster parents into adoptive parents were sociocultural (e.g., foster parents believed that they were too old to adopt or the children were too old to be adopted). As research with kinship caregivers reveals, some of this reluctance to adopt can be remedied [Testa et al. 1996]. For example, adoption is usually seen as something that is normatively appropriate only for young children and childless couples. When suitable counseling is provided, people are often willing to overlook these age-graded norms.

A more serious obstacle in the case of professional foster care is the understandable hesitancy of most foster parents to forfeit their professional status in favor of accepting adoptive responsibility for the children in their care. Income from the professional foster care program constitutes the sole source of household income for 80% of the foster parents in the PFC program, and it constitutes over one-half of the income for the remaining parents. If these foster parents were to adopt, they would lose their annual salary from the agency because the children would no longer be in publicly fundable foster care. Only the boarding payment would be eligible for conversion into an ongoing adoption subsidy that could be funded by the state. Without a doubt, the salaried position of the professional foster parent erects a financial obstacle to adoption that is much steeper than the usual financial obstacles to adoption in kinship and regular foster care.

The clash between professional interests and family commitments is precisely the concern that critics of the trend have voiced. Short of removing the children, the only solutions to this dilemma that preserve the status quo require either keeping alive the possibility of family reunification or demonstrating that the children's emotional or behavioral needs require ongoing professional involvement. The original evaluation indicated that foster parents in the PFC program were more likely to count family reunification as a viable permanency plan than the official state plan recorded for the children. One-third of children's officials records state that return home is not an option and the foster parents are either unable to assess the likelihood that the children will remain with them until they are adults or rate the chances as fair to very poor. It is these children who are left most in limbo in this professional foster care model.

Conclusion

The answer to the question posed by the title of this article is a qualified yes: professional foster care is an option worthy of future development. It accomplishes what many regular and specialized programs are unable to do in terms of stability, sibling placement, and community-based care. In comparison to regular family foster care, which returned only 7% of the children in state custody to their biological parents, the PFC program did better — almost twice the proportion of children (13%) returned home. The qualification in the answer arises from concern regarding the children who are not going home. PFC does not provide a permanent solution for them. During a time when welfare reform is eliminating financial assistance to needy parents who stay at home to care for their children, it is difficult to justify paying vastly greater sums of money to professional foster parents for stay-at-home family foster care.

Professional foster care makes economic and programmatic sense in a context of high rates of family reunification. The future of professional foster care depends on agencies working promptly and intensively with biological families to overcome multiple obstacles. If the conditions for reunification cannot be met within a reasonable period, it is incumbent upon agencies to work with biological parents, extended family, and other supportive networks to make alternative, legally permanent living arrangements that safeguard the best interests of the children.◆

References

Barth, R. P., Courtney, M., Berrick, J. D., & Albert, V. (1994). *From child abuse to permanency planning*. New York: Aldine De Gruyer.

Breckinridge, S. P. (1939). *The Illinois poor law and its administration*. Chicago: University of Chicago Press.

Chamberlain, P., Moreland, S., & Reid, K. (1992). Enhanced services and stipends for foster parents: Effects on retention rates and outcomes for children. *Child Welfare, 71*, 387–401.

Charen, M. (1997, October 6). Foster care repair. *Washington Times*.

Hamilton, W. (1964). The genetical evolution of social behavior I, II. *Journal of Theoretical Biology, 7*, 7–52.

Hasci, T. (1996). From indenture to family foster care: A brief history of child placing. In

E. P. Smith & L. A. Merkel–Holguin (Eds.), *A history of child welfare*. New Brunswick, NJ: Transaction Publishers.

Kahn, A. J., & Kammerman, S. B. (1990). Social services for children, youth and families in the United States. *Children and Youth Services Review, 1&2*, 1–180.

Lemay, R. (1991). Against the professionalization of foster care: An essay. *The Social Worker, 59*, 101–104.

Meyer, C. H. (1985). A feminist perspective on foster family care: A redefinition of the categories. *Child Welfare, 64*, 249–258.

Smith, E. P., & Gutheil, R. H. (1988). Successful foster parent recruiting: A voluntary agency effort. *Child Welfare, 67*, 137–146.

Tatara, T. (1998). Child substitute care flow data for FY 96, along with the U.S. child substitute care population trends. *VCIS Research Notes No. 14*. Washington, DC: American Public Welfare Association,

Testa, M. F., Rolock, N., & Werge, E. (1998). *Jane Addams Hull House Association Neighbor to Neighbor Program Evaluation*. Chicago: School of Social Service Administration.

Testa, M. F., Shook, K. L., Cohen, L., & Woods, M. (1996). Permanency planning options for children in formal kinship care. *Child Welfare, 75*, 451–470.

Thornton, J. L. (1991). Permanency planning for children in kinship foster homes. *Child Welfare, 70*, 593–601.

U.S. General Accounting Office. (1989). *Foster parents: Recruiting and pre-service practices need evaluation*. GAO/HRD-89-86. Washington, DC: Author.

Ward, M. (1984). Sibling ties in foster care and adoption planning. *Child Welfare, 63*, 321–330.

Zelizer, Z. A. (1985). *Pricing the priceless child: The changing social value of children*. New York: Basic Books.

Completing the Evaluation Triangle for the Next Century: Measuring Child "Well-Being" in Family Foster Care

7

Sandra J. Altshuler and James P. Gleeson

In recent years, success in family foster care has been evaluated by examining indicators of two goals of the child welfare system: permanency and safety. Systematic measures of child well-being have not been incorporated into the administrative databases that are used for case monitoring and evaluation. This article describes how child well-being has been conceptualized and measured in research on family foster care, and discusses the essential dimensions that should be included in a useful measure of child well-being. Challenges in incorporating measures of child well-being into ongoing evaluations of family foster care are discussed.

Sandra J. Altshuler, Ph.D., is Assistant Professor, School of Social Work, University of Illinois at Urbana-Champaign, Urbana, IL. James P. Gleeson, Ph.D., is Associate Professor, Jane Addams College of Social Work, University of Illinois at Chicago, Chicago, IL.

125

W e found no means being used or proposed for assessing, at specific intervals, the extent of change in and adequacy of a child's situation… The evaluations by local child welfare officials were primarily concerned with areas such as maintenance of case files, service planning, and service delivery… We believe that the effectiveness of any assistance program must be expressed in terms relative to the well–being of the program's target population. [USDHEW 1976: 64, quoted in Magura & Moses 1986: 2]

More than 20 years ago, the U. S. General Accounting Office concluded that the existing mechanisms for evaluating effectiveness did not allow systematic examination of the well-being of children in the care and custody of the child welfare system. In 1980, Magura and Moses [1980] challenged the field to move beyond measures of case events to develop systematic measures of child well-being that could be used to assess changes in children's situations and functioning during their involvement with the child welfare system. The U.S. Children's Bureau has consistently stated that the three primary goals of child welfare services are the achievement of safety and protection, timely permanence, and child well-being [Williams 1998]. Logically, evaluations of success in child welfare would triangulate measures of these three goals to determine effectiveness of service. Despite these exhortations, success in family foster care has been evaluated in recent years by examining indicators of only two goals of the child welfare system: permanency and safety. As the 21st century approaches, little progress has been made in incorporating systematic measures of child well-being into ongoing evaluations of family foster care.

This article offers direction for incorporating measures of child well-being into evaluations of success for family foster care. It discusses the need for these measures and the reasons that they have not been incorporated into administrative databases, describes the ways that child well-being has been conceptualized and measured in research that has focused on children living in family foster care, and discusses the essential dimensions that should be included in a useful measure of child well-being. It concludes with a discussion of the challenges in incorporating measures of child well-being into ongoing evaluations of family foster care to guide policy and practice into the next century.

Background

Not surprisingly, efforts to incorporate systematic measures of child well-being into evaluations of family foster care have not been sustained. Growth and changes in family foster care caseloads have placed considerable demands on the child welfare system, diverting energies and resources to meet these demands. This caseload growth has occurred in an era of political conservatism, increased scrutiny of the child welfare system, and class action lawsuits designed to reform the system. The advent of increased accountability, expedited permanency, managed care, and outcome-based contracting has redefined the policy environment for the child welfare system and pushed it to produce self-evaluations that address these critical issues, but do not necessarily focus on the well-being of children in family foster care.

For example, measures of child well-being are not part of most child welfare administrative databases and are not usually included in regular evaluations of child welfare system performance and family foster care. Systematic measures of child well-being are rarely used to assess the current functioning of children while they are in family foster care or changes in their functioning as a result of receiving services. If measures of child well-being are included at all, they are not generally used to evaluate success in care, but rather to predict other case outcomes such as reunification, reentry, adoption (e.g., Courtney [1994]; Landsverk et al. [1996]) or adolescent readiness for independence (e.g., Mech [1994]).

Especially since the passage of the Adoption Assistance and Child Welfare Act of 1980 [P.L. 96–272], measures of success in family foster care have focused primarily on safety and timely permanence for children in care. The Adoption and Safe Families Act of 1997 [P. L. 105–89] places even greater demands on child welfare systems to focus their measures of success on timely permanence; its requirements are intended to shorten the length of time children spend in out-of-home care and increase the number of adoptions. The law also mandates that the Secretary of the U.S. Department of Health and Human Services develop a set of outcome measures that state and local child welfare agencies can use to assess performance [42 U.S.C. § 679b].

Although P.L. 105-89 provides an opportunity to develop measures of child well-being and requires that these measures be incorporated into routine evaluations of performance, considerable reluctance to include child-well being as a performance indicator can be expected. There are good reasons for the absence of child well-being measures from child welfare monitoring and evaluation systems. First, child well-being is more difficult to define and measure than changes in case status (reunification, adoption, length of time in care, etc.) or confirmation of child maltreatment reports. Second, some child welfare agencies are understandably reluctant to measure child well-being. By the time children are taken into protective custody, their well-being has already worsened through exposure to increasingly harmful conditions that are beyond the control of the child welfare system. Nonetheless, expectations that the child welfare system will "fix" these children are very high. Systematically measuring child well-being may result in expanding the mandate for child welfare systems, despite the difficulties most systems are already experiencing in meeting the current mandates of child protection and permanency. Child welfare agencies may fear that systematic measures of child well-being will not only do little to improve the lives of children, but will also become another source of evidence that can be used to "prove" the ineffectiveness of the child welfare system.

Despite the risks, it is essential that measures of child well-being be routinely included in evaluations of child welfare agencies. As Magura and Moses [1986] have argued, measures of case status and reports of abuse and neglect are not adequate proxy measures for child well-being. Length of time in care and whether a child returns home or is adopted are not sufficient indicators of the child's perception of permanence, stability, and belonging. Confirmed child maltreatment reports tend to identify only the extreme cases and do not provide sensitive measures of a child's feelings of safety and security, nor do they provide accurate information on the development and functioning of children. Using systematic measures of well-being would allow child welfare systems to establish baseline data and compare trends in the well-being of children in family foster care over time.

Research on Child "Well-Being" in Family Foster Care

While systematic measures of child well-being have not been incorporated into the ongoing monitoring and evaluation systems of most child welfare systems, a body of research on child well-being has examined several domains of children's lives. These include overall functioning, health status, and school performance. The discussion that follows is accompanied by tables that highlight the domains and the various instruments used to measure these concepts.

Resilience, Coping, and Overall Functioning

Child well-being has often been assessed with various measures of overall functioning, including such domains as resilience and coping (see table 1). In 1955, Weinstein [1960] completed one of the earliest studies in child welfare that directly measured child well-being. He interviewed 61 children in out-of-home care of school age (5 to 14 years old) to identify factors that had an impact upon the children's well-being. The "Scale of Total Well-

TABLE 1

Designs and Instruments Used in Studies That Measured Resiliency, Coping, and Overall Functioning

Author	Design	Measurement Instruments
Weinstein 1960	Cross-sectional	Child Well-Being Scale Child Self-Concept Measure Questionnaire (Researcher-created)
Thorpe 1974, 1980	Cross-sectional	Child Well-Being Scale Child Self-Concept Measure Rutter Behavior Questionnaire Questionnaire (Researcher-created)
Fanshel & Shinn 1978	5-year longitudinal	see Tables 3-6 for specific measures of each domain of functioning
Fein et al. 1990	Cross-sectional	Child Functioning Scale (Researcher-created)

Dubowitz et al. 1993, 1994	Cross-sectional	see Tables 2, 3, 4, 6 for
		   specific measures of
		   each domain of functioning

Iglehart 1994	Cross-sectional	Measure of well-being (Researcher-created)

Being," designed for the study by a colleague of Weinstein's, operationally defined "child well-being" as the child's resiliency and coping ability assessed by caseworkers, as evidenced by the anchors at the extremes of the single-item, seven-point anchored scale he used in the study:

- *Extremely high total well-being.* This child will be able to handle anything. He'll make out fine regardless of the situation.
- *Extremely low total well-being.* This child will have difficulty in successfully weathering anything but the simplest type of situation. He will need constant protection in even ordinary life situations [Weinstein 1960: 65].

Thorpe [1974; 1980] replicated and expanded Weinstein's study by interviewing 121 English children in out-of-home care, their social workers, and 47 biological parents. Both Weinstein and Thorpe found low overall levels of resiliency and coping, but noted that higher levels of child well-being were associated with a clear understanding of the reasons for placement and consistent contact with biological parents.

Researchers have created global measures of overall functioning to evaluate levels of child well-being in family foster care. Fanshel and Shinn [1978] and Dubowitz and his colleagues [Dubowitz et al. 1993, 1994] assessed the functioning of 624 children in nonrelative care and 524 children in kinship care, respectively, in the following areas: emotional functioning (clinical assessments of psychological testing), behavioral characteristics, and school functioning (academic achievement, I.Q., and school behavior). Fanshel and Shinn included assessments of the child's adaptation to placement, while Dubowitz and colleagues also measured physical health. Both studies used multiple measures and sources (child; foster parents; biological parents, if possible; caseworkers; school personnel; and physicians [Dubowitz only]) and found that children in family foster care were functioning at levels below those displayed by children in the general population, although Fanshel and Shinn's longitudinal study demonstrated that children appear to benefit over time from placement in family foster care.

Other researchers have created composite measures to evaluate levels of child well-being in family foster care. Fein, Maluccio, and Kluger [1990] developed the Child Functioning Scale, which incorporated school achievement, behavior, emotions and development, and family adjustment based on caseworker and foster parent interviews. They concluded that the 779 children placed in long-term family foster care in their study appeared to be functioning well across all areas, supporting Fanshel and Shinn's earlier findings. Iglehart [1994] created a measure of well-being that combined caseworker ratings of mental health, behavior, and school functioning to determine an overall level of functioning to compare the well-being of adolescents placed in kinship versus nonrelative family foster care. She reported that teens in kinship care were functioning significantly better overall than their peers in nonrelative foster care.

Magura and Moses [1986] developed the Child Well-Being Scales, which consist of 43 anchored single-item scales that measure child functioning, parental functioning, and environmental conditions. These items can be used individually or combined in various ways to develop composite scores. Many of these items, however, are more relevant to the evaluation of home-based services than out-of-home care.

Physical Health

Physical health has been measured primarily through the identification of chronic or significant physical problems requiring medical attention found among children in out-of-home care. The prevalence of physical health problems has been assessed, without the use of control groups, through medical record reviews or through physical examinations by medical personnel of cross-sectional samples of children in care living primarily in major urban cities. Many researchers have found that children placed in family foster care have significant deficits in their health status compared to the general pediatric/adolescent population (see table 2) [Chernoff et al. 1994; Dubowitz et al. 1994; DuRousseau et al. 1991; Halfon et al. 1995; Hill et al. 1990; Hochstadt et al. 1987; Larsson et al. 1986; Lindsay et al. 1993; Moffat et al. 1985; Schor 1982; Simms 1991; Swire & Kavaler 1977]. For example, according to government reports, approximately 20% of all children in out-of-home care nationally exhibited some type of disability in 1985, as compared to 16% of children in the general pediatric population [Hill et al. 1990]. Concern also has been expressed regarding the lack of medical care being received for these conditions [American Academy of Pediatrics 1993; Horwitz et al. 1994; Schor 1989; Simms 1991].

Pediatricians who conducted physical exams in cross-sectional studies diagnosed 45% to 80% of children in family foster care as

TABLE 2

Designs and Instruments Used in Studies That Measured Physical Health

Author	Design	Measurement Instruments
Chernoff et al. 1994	Cross-sectional	Medical Records Review
Dubowitz et al. 1994	Cross-sectional	Medical Records Review
		Physical Exams by Pediatricians
DuRousseau et al. 1991	Cross-sectional	Medical Records Review
		Dietary Assessment by Nurses
		Physical Exams by Pediatricians
Halfon et al. 1995	Cross-sectional	Medical Records Review
		Physical Exams by Pediatricians
Hill et al. 1990	Cross-sectional	Questionnaire
		(Researcher-created)
Hochstadt et al. 1987	Cross-sectional	Medical Records Review
		Physical Exams by Pediatricians
Horwitz et al. 1994	Cross-sectional	Physical Exams by Pediatricians
Larsson et al. 1986	Cross-sectional	Case Records Review
Swire & Kavaler 1977	Cross-sectional	Medical Records Review
		Physical Exams by Pediatricians
Lindsay et al. 1993	Cross-sectional	Health screening by
		public health nurse
Moffat et al. 1985	Cross-sectional	Medical Records Review
		Physical Exams by Pediatricians
		Child Behavior Checklist
		Rutter's Teacher
		Questionnaire (Behavior)
Schor 1982	Cross-sectional	Medical Records Review

having chronic or significant physical problems requiring further medical attention or as lacking immunizations [Dubowitz et al. 1994; Halfon et al. 1995; Hochstadt et al. 1987; Moffat et al. 1985; Schor 1982; Swire & Kavaler 1977]. Each of these studies concluded that children living in family foster care suffer chronic health problems in excess of standards established for children in the general pediatric population. Many of these researchers noted, however, that these rates are similar to those found in studies of children from comparable socioeconomic situations [Schor 1982; Swire & Kavaler 1977]. One interesting finding among children in kinship foster care was the significant prevalence of obesity, not found in the nonrelative family foster care population but found in children in seriously economically disadvantaged families, and the "surprisingly infrequent" occurrence of certain maladies often assumed to be psychosomatic (headaches, stomachaches, enuresis, encopresis) [Dubowitz et al. 1994: 91].

Mental Health

Researchers have assessed the mental health status of children living in family foster care using measures of cognitive functioning, developmental delay, behavioral functioning, emotional or psychosocial functioning, or combinations thereof.

Cognitive functioning and developmental delay. Table 3 highlights the methods and instruments used to measure cognitive functioning and developmental delay. Two trends emerge from the studies that have assessed the cognitive functioning of children in care. First, upon entry into care, children in family foster care have scored approximately ten points below the normed populations of children on I.Q. tests, with minority children and children from lower socioeconomic levels scoring significantly lower [Dubowitz et al. 1994; Dumaret 1985; Fanshel & Shinn 1978; Fox & Arcuri 1980]. Second, Fanshel and Shinn demonstrated that changes in I.Q. scores over a five-year period were significantly correlated with ethnicity. Both African American and Puerto Rican children in family foster care achieved significant advances in I.Q., while the I.Q. scores of Caucasian children declined, if they remained in care for at least two years [Fanshel & Shinn 1978].

Other researchers have addressed the prevalence of developmental delays in children living in family foster care [Halfon et al. 1995; Hochstadt et al. 1987; Horwitz et al. 1994; Klee et al. 1997]. Almost 53% of 272 children under the age of 7 in one study [Horwitz et al. 1994] and 77% of 125 children under the age of 5 in another [Klee et al. 1997] displayed one or more developmental problems during their initial assessment. Dubowitz and col-

TABLE 3
Designs and Instruments Used in Studies That Measured Mental Health: Cognitive Ability and Developmental Delay

Author	Design	Measurement Instruments
Fanshel & Shinn 1978	5-year longitudinal	WISC Cattell Infant Scale Minnesota Preschool Scale
Fox & Arcuri 1980	Cross-sectional	WISC-R, WPPSI, WAIS (all Weschler I.Q. tests, age dependent)
Halfon et al. 1995	Cross-sectional	Connecticut Infant-Toddler Developmental Assessment Denver Developmental Screening Early Language Millstone Scale Slosson Intelligence Tests Developmental Test of VMI Peabody Picture Vocabulary Test-R Vineland Adaptive Behavior Scales
Hochstadt et al. 1987	Cross-sectional	Vineland Adaptive Behavior Scale Louisville Behavior Checklist Denver Developmental Screening
Horwitz et al. 1994	Cross-sectional	Connecticut Infant-Toddler Development Assessment Battelle Developmental Inventory (Preschool Language Scale only) Peabody Picture Vocabulary Test-R
Klee et al. 1997	Cross-sectional (Phase one of longitudinal study)	Bayley Scales of Infant Development
Dubowitz et ai. 1994	Cross-sectional	Cognitive Abilities Test (group-administered) Questionnaire (Researcher-created)

leagues also found that almost half of the children they were able to assess in their study were rated by their teachers as having specific skill deficits in problem solving and reasoning [Dubowitz et al. 1994].

Behavioral disturbance. Researchers often use standardized assessment instruments in both cross-sectional and longitudinal analyses (table 4) to demonstrate greater frequency and intensity of behavioral problems (e.g., attention-seeking behaviors, aggression, delinquency) among children in family foster care, as compared to children of similar age, gender, and race not placed into care [Berrick et al. 1994; Dubowitz et al. 1993; Fanshel et al. 1990; Fanshel & Shinn 1978; Garland et al. 1996; Glisson 1996; Hochstadt et al. 1987; Hulsey & White 1989; Iglehart 1994; Lambert et al. 1977; Landsverk et al. 1996; Marcus 1991; Pardeck 1983; Rock et al. 1988; Runyan & Gould 1985a; Wolkind & Rutter 1973]. Recent studies found that children living in both nonrelative and kinship foster care had significantly greater behavioral problems than children in the general population [Berrick et al. 1994; Glisson 1996; Iglehart 1994; Landsverk et al. 1996]. Behavioral problems have been positively associated with such factors as the number of placements a child has experienced [Marcus 1991; Runyan & Gould 1985a], marital instability of the biological parents [Hulsey & White 1989], infrequent parental visiting [Fanshel & Shinn 1978], placement due to abuse, and the child's gender [Dubowitz et al. 1993].

Emotional or psychosocial adjustment. Table 5 highlights the methods and instruments used to measure emotional disturbance. Estimates of the prevalence of emotional disturbance (e.g., withdrawal, anxiety, depression, somatic complaints, difficulties with attachment) among children living in family foster care range from 25% to 96% [Fanshel & Shinn 1978; Frank 1980; Garland et al. 1996; Gil & Bogart 1982; Hulsey & White 1989; Landsverk et al. 1996; Larsson et al. 1986; Marcus 1991; McIntyre & Keesler 1986;

TABLE 4
Designs and Instruments Used in Studies That Measured Mental Health: Behavioral Functioning

Author	Design	Measurement Instruments
Berrick et al. 1994	Cross-sectional	Behavior Problems Index
Dubowitz et al. 1993	Cross-sectional	Child Behavior Checklist ("CBCL")
Fanshel & Shinn 1978	5-year longitudinal	Child Behavior Characteristics Form
Fanshel et al. 1990	Retrospective longitudinal	Case Records Review
Garland et al. 1996	Cross-sectional	CBCL
Gil & Bogart 1982	Cross-sectional	Original Behavior Checklist
Glisson 1996	Cross-sectional	CBCL
Hulsey & White 1989	Cross-sectional	CBCL
Iglehart 1994	Cross-sectional	Questionnaire (Researcher-created)
Lambert et al. 1977	11-year longitudinal	Bristol Social Adjustment Guide Rutter Behavior Questionnaire (Researcher-modified)
Landsverk et al. 1996	6-month longitudinal	CBCL
Marcus 1991	Cross-sectional	CBCL
Pardeck 1983	Cross-sectional	Case Records Review (U.S. data)
Rock et al. 1988	Cross-sectional	Problem Behavior Scale of the Scales of Independent Behavior (Researcher-modified)
Runyan & Gould 1985a	Matched cohort	Juvenile court records
Wolkind & Rutter 1973	Cross-sectional	Questionnaire (Researcher-created)

Schor 1982; Swire & Kavaler 1977; Stein et al. 1996; Timberlake & Verdieck 1987; Thompson & Fuhr 1992], with two studies suggesting that children living in kinship foster care have lower rates of emotional disturbance than children living in nonrelative foster care [Iglehart 1994; Landsverk et al. 1996]. The wide range may be attributable to differences in measurement and design across these studies.

TABLE 5

Designs and Instruments Used in Studies That Measured Mental Health: Emotional/Psychosocial Functioning

Author	Design	Measurement Instruments
Fanshel & Shinn 1978	5-year longitudinal	Projective Tests (Draw-A-Person, Draw-A-Family, Michigan Picture Test)
		Questionnaire (Researcher-created)
Frank 1980	Retrospective, 5-year longitudinal	Rating scale of psychosocial problems (Researcher-created)
Garland et al. 1996	6-month longitudinal	Questionnaire (Reseacher-created)
Gil & Bogart 1982	Cross-sectional	Coopersmith Self-Esteem Inventory
		Parks Career Role Inventory
		Questionnaire (Researcher-created)
Halfon et al. 1992	Cross-sectional	Medicaid records review (mental health)
Hulsey & White 1989	Cross-sectional	CBCL
Iglehart 1994	Cross-sectional	Questionnaire (Researcher-created)
Swire & Kavaler 1977	Cross-sectional	Psychiatric screening
		Psychological clinical examination
Landsverk et al. 1996	6-month longitudinal	Case Records Review/ Rating scale (Researcher-created)
		CBCL (see "Behavior Functioning")
Marcus 1991	Cross-sectional	CBCL
		Rating scale of coping mechanisms (Researcher-created)
McIntyre & Keesler 1986	Cross-sectional	CBCL
Stein et al. 1996	Cross-sectional	Standardized Clinical Information System
Takayama et al. 1994	Cross-sectional	Medicaid Records Review (mental health)
Thompson & Fuhr 1992	Cross-sectional	CBCL
		Eysenck Personality Questionnaire
		Children's Depression Inventory
		Culture-Free Self-Esteem Inventory
		Review of Case Records
Timberlake & Verdieck 1987	Cross-sectional	Psychosocial Functioning Inventory (Researcher-created)

The cross-sectional studies that assessed the prevalence of emotional disturbance through nonstandardized means, such as psychiatric screenings, projective tests, and researcher-created rating scales, have produced the highest estimates of children in nonrelative foster care with emotional disturbances [Frank 1980; Marcus 1991; Swire & Kavaler 1977]. The longitudinal and cross-sectional studies that assessed the prevalence of emotional disturbance through standardized instruments found lower, but still significant, rates of pathology, and generally concluded that significantly higher numbers of children in nonrelative foster care than in the normed population demonstrated clinical levels of emotional disturbance [Fanshel & Shinn 1978; Gil & Bogart 1982; Landsverk et al. 1996; McIntyre & Keesler 1986; Stein et al. 1996; Thompson & Fuhr 1992]. Other researchers have used mental health service utilization to assess levels of emotional disturbance in children living in family foster care [Halfon et al. 1992; Takayama et al. 1994; Garland et al. 1996], despite its methodological challenges.

School Performance

Researchers of family foster care have frequently used school performance as an indicator of child well-being (see table 6), apparently because it is considered to be more "objective" than worker, parent, or child reports [Heath et al. 1994; Runyan & Gould 1985b]. Results from several studies have concluded that children in family foster care demonstrate significantly lower achievement and lower performance in school, compared to normed expectations [Berrick et al. 1994; Canning 1974; Dubowitz et al. 1994; Fanshel et al. 1990; Fanshel & Shinn 1978; Goerge et al. 1992; Health et al. 1994; Runyan & Gould 1985b; Smucker et al. 1996; Wolkind & Rutter 1973]. The conclusions were based primarily upon standardized achievement tests and school cumulative records, which schools maintain for all students. Compared to other children in similar classes, children in family foster care consistently perform at and are placed below age-appropriate grade levels, demonstrate inappropriate school-related behaviors more frequently, have poorer attendance records, and have higher retention rates. Two studies noted that significantly more children in nonrelative family foster care, when compared to those in kinship care, had repeated at least one grade or were enrolled in special education [Berrick et al. 1994; Goerge et al. 1992].

In assessing the impact of long-term family foster care placement on school performance, three longitudinal studies yielded conflicting results. Using only the standardized group test results for 114 children in nonrelative family foster care and 106 cohort comparison children, Runyan and Gould [1985b] found that over a three-year period, once children are placed in family foster care, their attendance significantly improved, although their performance did not. In contrast, studies by Heath and colleagues [1994] of 49 children in care in England and Fanshel and Shinn [1978] of 524 children in care in New York City found that overall school performance had, in fact, improved significantly over three- and five-year periods, respectively. The latter studies included individually administered standardized tests, not only group tests administered to all students in a class.

The Challenge of Incorporating Measures of Child "Well-Being" in Evaluation

The failure to incorporate systematic measures of child well-being into administrative databases used to monitor and evaluate family foster care cannot be blamed on an inability to measure this construct. Numerous research efforts have measured and examined the well-being of children in family foster care. Child well-being has been operationalized using global measures of resiliency, coping, and overall functioning, as well as individual or composite measures of physical health, mental health, and school performance. Mental health functioning has been assessed with measures of cognitive, emotional, and behavioral functioning.

TABLE 6
Designs and Instruments Used in Studies That Measured School Performance

Author	Design	Measurement Instruments
Berrick et al, 1994	Cross-sectional	Questionnaire (Researcher-created)
Canning 1974	Cross-sectional	Teacher & student interviews (Researcher-created)
Heath et al, 1994	Cohort, 3-year longitudinal	NFER's EH2 test (reading) BPVS (vocabulary) NFER's BM test (math)
Fanshel & Shinn 1978	5-year longitudinal	Rating Scale for Pupil Adjustment National achievement test scores School records (attendance, behavior)
Fanshel et al. 1990	Retrospective longitudinal	Case Records Review
Goerge et al. 1992	Cross-sectional	Case record & school record database
Runyan & Gould 1985b	Cross-sectional	Cumulative Folders (school records) National achievement test scores
Dubowitz et al. 1994	Cross-sectional	California Achievement Tests (group)
Smucker et al. 1996	Cross-sectional	School Records Questionnaire (Researcher-created)
Wolkind & Rutter 1973	Cross-sectional	Questionnaire (Researcher-created)

Creating or selecting common measures of child well-being in family foster care poses a formidable challenge. Dimensions of child well-being are of varying importance at different ages. At a minimum, measures of child well-being of infants and pre-school-age children must include assessments of their health, cognitive development, and behavioral functioning. For older children, measures of school performance, mental health, and resilience and coping should be added.

Repeated observations and multiple sources of data should be included to address the situational variances in functioning. For example, caseworkers might complete selected Child Well-Being Scales [Magura & Moses 1986] while the caregiver, teacher, and/or child might complete the Child Behavior Checklist [Achenbach 1981]. Standardized health and education reports like the San Diego computerized health and education passport [Lindsay et al. 1993] could be completed during regular health exams and school staffings and would be helpful in tracking child health and school performance over time. In addition, measures of resilience and coping could be completed by persons close enough to the child to know the child well, such as caseworkers and caregivers. Former and current children in family foster care also stress the importance of incorporating children's perceptions into measures of child well-being [Festinger 1983; Gil & Bogart 1982; Rest & Watson 1984]. Therefore, measures of child well-being should include the child's perceptions of safety, acceptance, permanence, stability, and belonging.

Research on the well-being of children in family foster care has primarily used cross-sectional designs, comparing the functioning of children in family foster care to that of children in the general population or from comparable socioeconomic backgrounds. Cross-sectional designs, however, are not effective for evaluating changes in the well-being of children that occur over the time they spend in family foster care and in the years that follow. Longitudinal designs are the only way to detect improvement or deterioration in child functioning. When longitudinal designs have been used to assess changes in child functioning, the benefits of family foster care have been demonstrated through improvements in health, intellectual, or school functioning. Repeated measures of child well-being that are systematically administered throughout a child's career in family foster care are essential if improvements and deterioration in child well-being are to be examined effectively.

For measures of child well-being to be useful, they must be easy to use and caseworkers must have the time to complete them. Caseworkers are already overburdened with paperwork demands. Currently, information about the well-being of children in family foster care, if it is part of the case record, is included primarily in narrative reports. If the child welfare system could develop a comprehensive, easy-to-use evaluative tool that incorporates brief standardized measures of child well-being across domains, these measures could replace much of the narrative reporting that is required and could be easily included in administrative databases. The San Diego County computerized health and education passport [Lindsay et al. 1993] may be the best model for accomplishing this formidable task.

The challenge for the next century is even more complicated than developing valid, easy-to-use, relatively short, comparable measures of child well-being. It is also political. Leadership is needed to influence local child welfare systems and juvenile court systems to accept common measures of child well-being in lieu of existing narrative reporting. Federal, state, and local child welfare agencies need to eliminate any paperwork that is not essential to ensuring or assessing the permanence, safety, or well-being of children in family foster care.

Often what is measured shapes our definition of success. If measures of child well-being are not routinely collected and recorded, the impact of new permanency initiatives, managed care, and outcome-based contracting will be judged solely by caseload size, length of service, and cost. Identifying, creating, and agreeing upon common measures of child well-being that can be incorporated into administrative databases, along with measures of permanency and safety, is no small task. It is essential that we undertake this challenge to complete the evaluation triangle, to provide an understanding of the direct impact on children of family foster care policies and practices, and to shape child welfare policy and practice in the next century.◆

References

Achenbach, T. M. (1981). *Child behavior checklist for ages 4–16*. Burlington, VT: University Associates in Psychiatry.

American Academy of Pediatrics, Committee on Early Childhood, Adoption and Dependent Care. (1993). Developmental issues in foster care for children. *Pediatrics, 91,* 1007–1009.

Berrick, J. D., Barth, R. P., & Needell, B. (1994). A comparison of kinship foster homes and foster family homes: Implications for kinship foster care as family preservation. *Children and Youth Services Review, 16,* 33–63.

Canning, R. (1974). School experiences of foster children. *Child Welfare, 53,* 582–586.

Chernoff, R., Combs-Orme, T., Risley-Curtiss, C., & Heisler, A. (1994). Assessing the health status of children entering foster care. *Pediatrics, 93,* 594–601.

Courtney, M. E. (1994). Factors associated with the reunification of foster children with their families. *Social Service Review, 68*(1), 81–108.

Dubowitz, H., Feigelman, S., Harrington, D., Starr, R., Zuravin, S., & Sawyer, R. (1994). Children in kinship care: How do they fare? *Children and Youth Services Review, 16,* 85–106.

Dubowitz, H., Zuravin, S., Starr, R. H., Feigelman, S., & Harrington, D. (1993). Behavior problems of children in kinship care. *Journal of Developmental and Behavioral Pediatrics, 14,* 386–393.

Dumaret, A. (1985). IQ, scholastic performance and behaviour of sibs raised in contrasting environments. *Journal of Child Psychology and Psychiatry and Allied Disciplines, 26,* 553–580.

DuRousseau, P. C., Maquette, M. E., & Disbrow, D. (1991). Children in foster care: Are they at nutritional risk? *Journal of American Dietetic Association, 91,* 83–85.

Fanshel, D., Finch, S. J., & Grundy, J. F. (1990). *Foster children in life–course perspective.* New York: Columbia University Press.

Fanshel, D., & Shinn, E. B. (1978). *Children in foster care.* New York: Columbia University Press.

Fein, E., Maluccio, A. N., & Kluger, M. (1990). *No more partings: An examination of long–term foster family care.* Washington, DC: Child Welfare League of America, Inc.

Festinger, T. (1983). *No one ever asked us… A postscript to foster care*. New York: Columbia University Press.

Fox, M., & Arcuri, K. (1980). Cognitive and academic functioning in foster children. *Child Welfare, 59*, 491–496.

Frank, G. (1980). Treatment needs of children in foster care. *American Journal of Orthopsychiatry, 50*, 256–263.

Garland, A. F., Landsverk, J. L., Hough, R. L., & Ellis–MacLeod, E. (1996). Type of maltreatment as a predictor of mental health service use for children in foster care. *Child Abuse and Neglect, 20*, 675–688.

Gil, E., & Bogart, K. (1982). Foster children speak out: A study of children's perceptions of foster care. *Children Today, 11*, 7–9.

Glisson, C. (1996). Judicial and service decisions for children entering state custody: The limited role of mental health. *Social Service Review*, 257–281.

Goerge, R. M., VanVoorhis, J., Grant, S., Casey, K., & Robinson, M. (1992). Special-education experiences of foster children: An empirical study. *Child Welfare, 71*, 419–437.

Halfon, N., Berkowitz, G., & Klee, L. (1992). Mental health service utilization by children in foster care in California. *Pediatrics, 89*, 1238–1244.

Halfon, N., Mendonca, A., & Berkowitz, G. (1995). Health status of children in foster care: The experience of the Center for the Vulnerable Child. *Archives of Pediatric and Adolescent Medicine, 149*, 386–392.

Heath, A. F., Colton, M. J., & Aldgate, J. (1994). Failure to escape: A longitudinal study of foster children's educational attainment. *British Journal of Social Work, 24*, 241–260.

Hill, B. K., Hayden, M. F., Lakin, K. C., Menke, J., & Amado, A. R. N. (1990). State-by-state data on children with handicaps in foster care. *Child Welfare, 69*, 447–462.

Hochstadt, N. J., Jaudes, P. K., Zimo, D. A., & Schachter, J. (1987). The medical and psychosocial needs of children entering foster care. *Child Abuse and Neglect, 11*, 53–62.

Horwitz, S. M., Simms, M. D., & Farrington, R. (1994). Impact of developmental problems on young children's exits from foster care. *Journal of Developmental and Behavioral Pediatrics, 15*, 105–110.

Hulsey, T. C., & White, R. (1989). Family characteristics and measures of behavior in foster and nonfoster children. *American Journal of Orthopsychiatry, 59*, 502–509.

Iglehart, A. (1994). Kinship foster care: Placement, service and outcome issues. *Children and Youth Services Review, 16*, 107–122.

Klee, L., Kronstadt, D., & Zlotnick, C. (1997). Foster care's youngest: A preliminary report. *American Journal of Orthopsychiatry, 67*, 290–299.

Lambert, L., Essen, J., & Head, J. (1977). Variations in behaviour ratings of children who have been in care. *Journal of Child Psychology and Psychiatry and Allied Disciplines, 18*, 335–346.

Landsverk, J., Davis, I., Ganger, W., Newton, R., & Johnson, I. (1996). Impact of child psychosocial functioning on reunification from out–of–home placement. *Children and Youth Services Review, 18*, 447–462.

Larsson, G., Bohlin, A., & Stenbacka, M. (1986). Prognosis of children admitted to institutional care during infancy. *Child Abuse and Neglect, 10*, 361–368.

Lindsay, S., Chadwick, D., Landsverk, J., & Pierce, E. (1993). A computerized health and education passport for children in out–of–home care: The San Diego model. *Child Welfare, 72*, 581–594.

Magura, S., & Moses, B. S. (1980). Outcome measurement in child welfare. *Child Welfare, 59*, 595–606.

Magura, S., & Moses, B. S. (1986). *Outcome measures for child welfare services: Theory and applications.* Washington, DC: Child Welfare League of America, Inc.

Marcus, R. F. (1991). The attachments of children in foster care. *Genetic, Social and General Psychology Monographs, 117*, 365–394.

McIntyre, A. E., & Keesler, T. Y. (1986). Psychological disorders among foster children. *Journal of Clinical Child Psychology, 15*, 297–303.

Mech, E. V. (Ed.). (1994). Preparing foster youth for adulthood. *Children and Youth Services Review (special issue), 16*.

Moffat, M. E. K., Peddie, M., Stulginskas, J., Pless, I. B., & Steinmetz, N. (1985). Health care delivery to foster children: A study. *Health and Social Work, 10*, 129–137.

Pardeck, J. T. (1983). An empirical analysis of behavioral and emotional problems of foster children as related to re–placement in care. *Child Abuse and Neglect, 7*, 75–78.

Rest, E. R., & Watson, K. W. (1984). Growing up in foster care. *Child Welfare, 63*, 291–308.

Rock, S. L., Flanzer, S. M., Bradley, R. H., & Pardeck, J. T. (1988). Frequency of maladaptive behavior in foster children. *Early Child Development and Care, 30*, 133–139.

Runyan, D. K., & Gould, C. L. (1985a). Foster care for child maltreatment: Impact on delinquent behavior. *Pediatrics, 75*, 562–568.

Runyan, D. K., & Gould, C. L. (1985b). Foster care for child maltreatment. II. Impact on school performance. *Pediatrics, 76*, 841–47.

Schor, E. L. (1982). The foster care system and health status of foster children. *Pediatrics, 69*, 521–528.

Schor, E. L. (1989). Foster care. *Pediatrics in Review, 10*, 209–216.

Simms, M. D. (1991). Foster children and the foster care system, part II: Impact on the child. *Current Problems in Pediatrics, 21*, 345–369.

Smucker, K. S., Kauffman, J. M., & Ball, D. W. (1996). School–related problems of special education foster care students with emotional or behavioral disorders: A comparison to other groups. *Journal of Emotional and Behavioral Disorders, 4*(1), 30–39.

Stein, E., Evans, B., Mazumdar, R., & Rae-Grant, N. (1996). The mental health of children in foster care: A comparison with community and clinical samples. *Canadian Journal of Psychiatry, 41*, 385–391.

Swire, M. R., & Kavaler, F. (1977). The health status of foster children. *Child Welfare, 56*, 635–653.

Takayama, J. I., Bergman, A. B., & Connell, F. A. (1994). Children in foster care in the state of Washington. *Journal of the American Medical Association, 271*, 1850–1855.

Thompson, A. H., & Fuhr, D. (1992). Emotional disturbance in fifty children in the care of a child welfare system. *Journal of Social Service Research, 15*, 95–112.

Thorpe, R. (1974). Mum and Mrs. So & So. *Social Work Today, 4*, 691–695.

Thorpe, R. (1980). The experiences of children and parents living apart. In J. Triseliotis (Ed.), *New developments in foster care and adoption* (pp. 85–100). London: Routledge & Kegan Paul.

Timberlake, E. M., & Verdieck, M. J. (1987). Psychosocial functioning of adolescents in foster care. *Social Casework*, 214–222.

Weinstein, E. A. (1960). *The self-image of the foster child*. New York: Russell Sage Foundation.

Williams, C. W. (1998, February). Opening plenary session. Fifth National Child Welfare Conference: *Strengthening Family and Community Commitment to Safety, Permanence, and Well-being of Children*. Arlington, VA.

Wolkind, S., & Rutter, M. (1973). Children who have been "in care": An epidemiological study. *Journal of Child Psychology and Psychiatry and Allied Disciplines, 14*, 97–105.

Starting Young: Improving the Health and Developmental Outcomes of Infants and Toddlers in the Child
8 Welfare System

Judith Silver, Paul DiLorenzo, Margaret Zukoski, Patricia E. Ross, Barbara J. Amster, and Diane Schlegel

The number of infants and toddlers entering out-of-home care has increased dramatically in the past few years, yet few published reports examine their needs. This article describes a collaborative, multidisciplinary developmental follow-up program for infants and toddlers that builds on the community-based family support model described in the Family to Family Foster Care Reform Initiative. The children's health and developmental status, as well as the program's effectiveness, are highlighted.

Judith Silver, Ph.D., is Assistant Professor of Pediatrics (Psychology); Patricia E. Ross, M.D., is Clinical Assistant Professor of Pediatrics; and Barbara J. Amster, M.D., is Assistant Professor of Pediatrics (Speech-Language Pathology), Medical College of Pennsylvania–Hahnemann School of Medicine, Philadelphia, PA. Paul DiLorenzo, ACSW, MLSP, is Special Assistant to the Deputy Secretary, Commonwealth of Pennsylvania Office of Children, Youth and Families, Harrisburg, PA. Margaret

Children are placed in family foster care when their parents cannot adequately care for them. The merits of foster care are frequently debated by both the public and professionals [Hornblower 1995; Schorr 1997; Smolowe 1995]. One concern involves the misguided notion that out-of-home care is an endpoint service that "rescues" children from their parents. Traditionally, placement in care involves a functional "divorce" of the children not only from their biological families, but also from their neighborhoods, schools, health care providers, and friends. For children with special medical needs or developmental problems, the absolute nature of this separation may have repercussions after reunification, when they return to parents who may be uninformed about their health care needs and inadequately prepared to provide appropriate care. As a result, the child's well-being is jeopardized and the family is again vulnerable to state-imposed dissolution.

In response to problems associated with traditional models of out-of-home care, the Annie E. Casey Foundation developed the Family to Family Foster Care Reform Initiative, which seeks to decrease the number of children in out-of-home care, the number of days spent in care, and the number of disrupted placements; and to enhance the ability of agencies to utilize data to support practice decisions [Annie E. Casey Foundation 1992].

In Pennsylvania, the state Department of Public Welfare and the Philadelphia Department of Human Services worked with several private child welfare agencies to redefine the provision of family foster care services to reflect the tenets of the Family to Family initiative. These agencies convened a group of community residents, foster parents, and professionals to develop a collaborative communitywide model of family support-based child

Zukoski, MSS, MLSP, is Policy Specialist, Children, Youth, and Family Council, Philadelphia, PA. Diane Schlegel, PT, B.S., is Physical Therapist, Starting Young Program, St. Christopher's Hospital for Children, Philadelphia, PA. Preparation of this article was supported by a grant to the first author by the Pew Charitable Trusts fund for local health and human services programs. The authors thank Lisa Cheever for her able assistance.

welfare services. Included in the group were representatives from the pediatrics department of a local medical school, who had previously developed a program to improve the health and developmental outcomes of infants and toddlers in out-of-home care. Infants and toddlers are the most dramatically expanding age group entering care [Carnegie Corporation 1994; Halfon & Klee 1987; Wulczyn & Goerge 1992]. Information on the needs of this cohort is crucial for program development in the next century.

This article reports on the Starting Young Program, a pediatric developmental follow-up program for infants and toddlers involved with the public child welfare agency. Starting Young was developed in response to the large number of children in out-of-home care who present with medical and developmental problems yet underutilize health care and early intervention (EI) services.

Health and Developmental Outcomes for Children in Out-of-Home Care

Due to the interactions of both medical and social risk factors, children entering out-of-home care experience higher rates of both acute and chronic medical conditions, developmental delays, and mental health problems than those found among the general population [Chernoff et al. 1994; Hochstadt et al. 1987; Simms 1989]. Typically, children entering care have histories of prenatal exposure to drugs or alcohol as well as experiences of neglect, abuse, and fragmented medical care [Schor 1982; Simms 1989].

Unfortunately, even after the children's placement in care, their health care needs are often neglected [Halfon et al. 1995; Moffat et al. 1985; Takayama et al. 1994]. Many do not receive adequate health supervision or preventative care such as immunizations. This lack of consistent adequate care and follow-up is especially problematic for children who need more than standard pediatric care, such as those in need of medical, allied health, EI, and mental health services [Frank 1980; Halfon et al. 1992; Halfon & Klee 1987; Hochstadt et al. 1987; Schor 1982]. Deficiencies in access to appropriate services are systemic, due to a lack of coordination among service providers responsible for the children's health and welfare [Frank 1980; Halfon & Klee 1987; Schor 1982]; minimal training for child welfare professionals regarding children's health and development [Halfon & Klee 1991]; high turnover among foster care workers [Simms & Halfon 1994]; and multiple changes in the children's placements, resulting in a change in their health care providers [Schor 1982; Simms & Halfon 1994]. Further complications involve issues unique to the child welfare system, such as the legal rights of the children's biological parents. In many states, immunizations, psychotherapy, EI therapies, and many medical procedures often cannot be provided to children in out-of-home care without the biological parents' consent, even when the state has legal custody. Delays in obtaining these services occur when biological parents cannot be located or when they refuse their consent. In these cases, a court order must be obtained, which results in additional delays for the child in need of services. Parental consent also is required to release medical, educational, and mental health records to those providing care to the children. The problems associated with issues of confidentiality and consent can impede a child's access to health care while in placement.

The impact of these problems is greatest on infants and toddlers. Children under 3 years of age are more vulnerable to the effects of disease, malnutrition, physical abuse, and emotional deprivation than those in any other age group. All of these insults can impede physical development and brain growth. Extensive research in infant development has confirmed that adequate nurturance in the earliest stages of life is critical to the child's future health, development, and emotional well-being [Drotar et al. 1980; Sameroff & Chandler 1975; Spitz 1945,1946]. The immature nervous systems of young children are more pliable and responsive to both stress and intervention during this period than during any other stage of life.

Indeed, the Education of the Handicapped Act Amendments

of 1986 (P.L. 99-457), which created a federal entitlement to EI services for children from birth until entry into elementary school, sought to capitalize on the extensive research and clinical observations about infants' capabilities [Teti & Gibbs 1990]. EI services include physical, occupational, and speech-language therapies; nutrition; special education services; and case management. Research has indicated that these services result in more favorable outcomes for children with delays due to both biological and social risk factors [Beckwith 1988; Birch & Gussow 1970; Dunst 1993; Infant Health and Development Program 1990; Sameroff 1993; Shonkoff & Hauser-Cram 1987; Sigman & Parmelee 1979]. Unfortunately, research documenting the use of EI services by children in out-of-home care is lacking [Spiker & Silver 1999]. In one study that evaluated young children in family foster care, 60% of those who had been identified as eligible for EI and had been in placement an average of six months were not enrolled in any therapeutic program [Simms 1989].

The literature reports on a limited but growing number of programs that seek to improve the early identification of the medical, developmental, and emotional needs of children in out-of-home care; the access of these children to timely intervention; and the coordination of these services for them. Simms and Halfon [1994] group most of these programs into two models: those that provide a centralized source of health care and developmental assessment [Blatt et al. 1997; Simms & Halfon 1994], and those that have decentralized programs that either support children from multiple communities or serve as an adjunct to the child's community-based primary health care provider [Halfon et al. 1995; Simms 1989]. Funding for such programs often depends on a patchwork of contracts, time-limited start-up grants, and *pro bono* agreements. The tenuous nature of programs dependent on such arrangements is well-known to child welfare professionals. The same problems found in the provision of health care services are encountered in devising other multidisciplinary programs to meet children's needs in ways not easily addressed through categorical funding streams [Davis & Caruso 1999; Klee & Kronstadt 1999; Peckham 1999].

Only a few published reports on the health and development of children in out-of-home care have focused on infants and preschoolers [U.S. GAO 1995; Halfon et al. 1995; Horowitz et al. 1994; Simms 1989]. This lack of recognition and understanding of the medical and developmental needs of these children by the adults responsible for their care can lead to adverse outcomes.

Program Background

The Starting Young Program is a multidisciplinary developmental follow-up diagnostic and referral service exclusively for children who are receiving services through the Philadelphia Department of Human Services (DHS). Located in the Department of Pediatrics of a teaching hospital, the evaluation team includes a pediatrician, child psychologist, speech-language pathologist, physical therapist, and pediatric social worker. To improve collaboration across multiple systems, the evaluation team is joined by a social worker from ChildLink (the county EI service coordination agency) who is authorized to complete an intake and individualized family service plan and to enroll children who qualify in community-based EI programs. Ongoing collaboration with child welfare personnel is assured by the inclusion of the child's foster care worker and foster parent in the intake and evaluation. Foster care workers are encouraged to invite the child's biological parents to attend the session, since helping parents maintain a relationship with their children is a key tenet of the Family to Family Initiative. Children who reside with their biological parents and receive in-home (IH) child welfare services are accompanied by their parent and IH worker. Most published reports on programs serving children in family foster care do not include those known to the child welfare system who remain in their parents' care and receive IH services. The Starting Young Program includes these high-risk families with the hope that its services will help prevent the child's placement into care. Also, many children experience placement changes, moving from IH services to out-of-home care, and eventually back to their families. Starting Young tracks the children for reevaluations, offering continuity in helping their foster and biological parents understand the child's medical and developmental needs and obtain appropriate services.

Although the Starting Young Program does not provide primary health care services, it serves as a resource to the workers and caregivers of infants and toddlers placed throughout the five county metropolitan area. Throughout the year, the program offers several training programs for child welfare professionals on children's health and development.

The program's primary goal is to improve the health and developmental outcomes of infants in the child welfare system by (1) identifying developmental and medical problems; (2) facilitating access to evaluations and intervention services; (3) establishing linkages between pediatric, child welfare, and EI agencies to improve coordination of services; (4) training child welfare personnel to identify infants with developmental and medical risk factors and access services for them; and (5) training medical students in multidisciplinary, collaborative models of service.

Program Description

Children up to 30 months old are referred to Starting Young by foster care or IH workers from more than 40 private agencies under contract to DHS, or by DHS personnel. The team social worker contacts both the worker and the child's caregiver (i.e., the biological parent or the foster parent) by phone to conduct the intake interview, and to identify any concerns regarding the child.

Children are accompanied to the evaluation by their caregiver and child welfare worker. The children are evaluated by members of the developmental team and examined by the pediatrician, with medical students observing. Feedback is provided to the caregiver and child welfare worker at the conclusion of the session and includes discussion of the child's pattern of strengths and needs, informal consultation on enhancing the child's development and behavior, and recommendations for additional services, if warranted. If the child is eligible for EI services, the ChildLink intake worker explains the child's federal entitlement and the range of available services. Once proper authorization is obtained, formal reports are sent to the child welfare agency, the DHS caseworker, and the caregiver. Children are reevaluated every six months until they reach 30 months of age, regardless of any changes in their placement status (such as discharge from out-of-home care).

The Starting Young Program is funded primarily through a grant from a private foundation, The Pew Charitable Trusts, which covers the direct services of the developmental specialists, as well as the administrative costs of the program. The Department of Pediatrics covers one-third of the social worker's time and supports the cost of the pediatrician, since the program serves as a special ambulatory clinic site for third-year medical students' pediatric rotations. Although Medicaid reimbursement (Title XIX funds) initially covered the cost of the children's pediatric evaluations, this form of revenue eroded over time with the increasing enrollment of the IH children into managed care health plans. As of July 1997, all children evaluated by the program were enrolled in compulsory managed health care programs for Medicaid-eligible recipients; thus, no reimbursement is received for their pediatric evaluations since the children are capitated to their primary health care provider within their health plan. Some of these managed care programs provide referrals for the speech-language evaluations. ChildLink supports the position of the EI intake worker through its contract with the county Office of Mental Retardation to provide centralized service coordination for EI eligible children and their families.

Results

Five hundred twenty-three (523) evaluations and reevaluations were conducted on 308 children between November 1992 and September 1997. The discussion here is limited to the children's initial evaluations. The program's sample of children proportionately reflects the ethnic makeup of all children younger than 31 months entering out-of-home care in Philadelphia County over a similar period of time (table 1).

The children came to the attention of child welfare authorities primarily due to parental substance abuse (53.6%), significant neglect (35.1%), and medical neglect (24.4%). Substandard housing or homelessness was a factor for many (22.7%). Abandonment (15.6%) and maternal mental illness (12.7%) also played an important role in the children's entry into the child welfare system. Physical abuse (8.8%), as well as the abuse of a sibling (9.4%), and sexual abuse (2.3%) were less prevalent reasons.*

Pediatric evaluations indicated that 22.1% of these children were underimmunized; 43.1% presented with an acute medical illness, and 60.3% had chronic conditions (table 2). Growth problems (identified as a weight for height ratio at or below the 10th percentile for age) were identified in 20.2% of the children (twice the expected rate found among the general population). The results of the developmental evaluations indicated that delays in language were the most frequent problem (57.1%), followed by those in cognitive (33.4%) and gross-motor (31.2%) domains.

Of the children evaluated by the pediatrician, 41.2% were referred to medical specialists for further evaluation and/or treatment. Nearly half (49.0%) of the children met the criteria for enrollment in EI services in Pennsylvania, a rate far surpassing the 10% to 12% expected among the general population of children [Baker 1989].

---

* Multiple reasons for entry into the system were documented for many children, thus the sum of percentages exceeds 100%.

TABLE 1
Demographic Characteristics

	Starting Young Program* (N = 308)		Philadelphia County** (N = 1,163)	
	N	%	N	%
Gender				
Male	175	56.8	608	52.3
Female	133	43.2	554	47.6
Ethnicity				
African American	244	79.2	859	73.9
Caucasian	27	8.8	57	4.9
Latino	22	7.1	50	4.3
Other	15	4.9	109	9.4
Placement Status				
Foster Care	182	59.1	1163	100
In-Home with Parent(s)	126	40.9	-	-

* Data are for all children seen in SY for initial evaluations between 11/1/92 - 8/30/97.
** Data are for all Philadelphia children 30 months and younger entering first foster care placement in 1995 and 1996 [Kutzler 1998].

Although the Starting Young Program was able to identify a large number of previously unknown and unmet needs among these children, its effectiveness depends on follow-through with its recommendations. The greatest follow-through involved enrollment in EI programs (83%), followed by updating immunizations (76%). Follow-through was poorest in obtaining additional medical evaluations (57%). Contributing to poor follow-through may be factors unique to the children's involvement in the child welfare system, such as a change in child welfare worker (37.0%); and a change in placement within 8 to 12 weeks after the evaluation (21.8%; see table 3).

Since 1992, more than 500 child welfare professionals have received training from Starting Young. Approximately 90% of the referrals to the developmental follow-up program originate from agencies that send personnel for the training.

TABLE 2

Prominent Medical Diagnoses and Prevalence of Developmental Delays

	Number of Children	%
Acute Medical Conditions (N = 267)[1]	*115*	*43.1*
Recurrent Otitis Media	34	12.7
(Middle ear infection)		
Dermatologic	46	17.2
Respiratory Infections	20	7.5
Chronic Medical Conditions (N = 267)[1]	*161*	*60.3*
Neuromuscular	61	22.9
Skeletal	21	7.9
Reactive Airway Disease (Asthma)	16	6.0
Developmental Delays[2]		
Speech-Language (N = 289)	176	57.1
Cognitive (N = 261)	103	33.4
Gross-Motor (N = 286)	96	31.2
Growth (N = 267)[3]	54	20.2

1. Forty-one (13.3%) of the total group were not examined due to physician's absence or child's extreme distress.
2. Based on children receiving a standard score <85 on the following measures: Preschool Language Scale, Third Edition [Zimmerman et al. 1992]; Receptive-Expressive Emergent Language Test, Second Edition [Bzoch & League 1991]; Bayley Scales of Infant Development [Bayley 1969]; Peabody Developmental Motor Scale [Folio & Fewell 1983].
3. Measured by pediatrician with weight for height ratio $\leq 10^{th}$ percentile.

Discussion

The high rate of medical problems and developmental delays identified in this group of children is stunning when compared to prevalence figures found among children in the general population, including those born into poverty. Previous studies of children in out-of-home care, however, have found similar results [Chernoff et al. 1994; U.S. GAO 1995; Halfon et al. 1995; Hochstadt et al. 1987; Moffat et al. 1985; Simms 1989]. All of the children evaluated in the Starting Young Program receive their ongoing health care elsewhere. The high incidence of pediatric subspe-

TABLE 3

Recommendations for Services and Obstacles to Care

Recommendations (N = 308)*	Number of Children	%
Early Intervention	151	49.0
Medical Specialists	127	41.2
Update Immunizations	68	22.1
Obstacles		
Change in Worker	114	37.0
Placement Change (N = 156)*	34	21.8

* Children seen for reevaluations 6-10 months after the initial SY evaluation.

cialty referrals raises questions about whether the children actually have a "medical home" where they are being seen on a regular basis and, if so, whether their needs are being identified.

The study reported here is one of the few to examine follow-through with different categories of services for young children in the child welfare system. There was excellent completion of referrals for EI services and updating immunizations. Easy access likely played a major role in assuring that these recommendations were followed, since Philadelphia offers neighborhood-based immunization outreach programs and EI. The poorest rate of follow-through involved recommendations for additional medical evaluations, which was similar to the rate identified by a study of foster care children in Baltimore [Chernoff et al. 1994]. In the current study, the obstacles to obtaining timely subspecialty medical evaluations may have been due to variables associated with the health care delivery system, the child welfare system, or a combination. Although the Philadelphia metropolitan area has several children's hospitals with subspecialty services, waiting lists are long. Some medical providers refused to accept standard general medical consent forms signed by biological parents when children were first placed in out-of-home care, thus delaying the children's access to care. Conversely, some children did not see medical specialists due to the turnover in social workers or changes in the child's placement, or because the worker believed there was no apparent urgency. Research indicates that even when recommendations for specialty medical evaluations have been identified as "urgent," many children in out-of-home care do not receive them within a reasonable time frame, if at all [Chernoff et al. 1994].

Due to concern about the limited compliance with medical referrals, follow-up inquiries by the team's social worker were implemented after the first year of the program's operation, resulting in a modest improvement in compliance. In cases where poor compliance with recommendations could jeopardize the child's health or well-being, Starting Young personnel actively advocated for the child by contacting DHS administrators, legal advocates, and other professionals who could be instrumental in assuring that the child received the needed services. Consequently, many of the children eventually completed the recommendations; those data, however, could not be included in the rate of follow-through reported here.

Conclusions

Nearly two decades after the implementation of the Adoption Assistance and Child Welfare Act of 1980 (P.L. 96-272), the problem of "foster care drift," in which children languish in care without a reasonable permanency plan, continues. With the passage of the Adoption and Safe Families Act of 1997 (P.L. 105-89) Congress once again has focused attention on establishing safe, permanent homes for children in a timely manner. Currently, toddlers with developmental delays and behavior problems often remain in family foster care longer and experience more failed placements than older children [Horowitz et al. 1994]. Comprehensive, multidisciplinary evaluations for young children, access to health care, and other interventions can improve the children's functioning and even their prognoses, as well as provide supports to foster and biological parents. These measures have an important role to play in reducing the number of failed placements and may serve as protective factors in preventing reentry into out-of-home care following reunification. The information provided by multidisciplinary developmental assessments is vital to meaningful permanency planning.

Although studies have indicated that interventions in the first three years of life have far-reaching implications for the future health and development of the child, child welfare agencies typically have not capitalized on this knowledge, despite the growing number of very young children entering out-of-home care. If family foster care is to be a meaningful intervention in the next century, it must integrate developmental services into the service plan of every child. Given the positive impact of EI services, all infants and toddlers in family foster care should be evaluated for eligibility and referred for enrollment soon after entering placement. Such evaluations are crucial even for infants without histories of maltreatment (such as those who entered care upon discharge from the newborn nursery) because of the profound impact that pre- and perinatal risk factors may have had upon the child's health and development.

Child welfare agencies should examine their policy and practice guidelines to assure timely access to both routine and specialty health care evaluations. Training for social workers, foster parents, and biological parents on the health and developmental needs of young children and on how to secure relevant, community-based services can offer additional supports to families and improve the children's outcomes.

Child welfare agencies also are encouraged to develop linkages with health care providers and EI agencies to improve communication and coordination of services, and develop intersystem educational opportunities to enhance these efforts. Effective child welfare practice demands linkages across many systems to ensure that the child and family receive services before, during, and following placement.

Simms and Halfon [1994] highlighted the need for a "research agenda" to examine obstacles to the adequate provision of health care services to children in out-of-home care, and the identification of effective models of health care service delivery for these children. The experiences of the Starting Young Program support the need for additional research focused on improving the outcomes for the youngest children. Without legislation mandating adequate and timely health care services, and without sufficient federal oversight and funding of such efforts, children in out-of-home care will continue to experience medical neglect [U.S. GAO 1995; Simms & Halfon 1994]. Armed with recent legislation and current research, child welfare professionals can be primed to better serve infants and toddlers in the 21st century.◆

References

Annie E. Casey Foundation. (1992). Family to family reconstructing foster care initiative. Greenwich, CT: Author.

Baker, C. (1989). *Education indicators*. National Center for Education Statistics, U.S. Department of Education. Washington, DC: U.S. Government Printing Office.

Bayley, N. (1969). *Bayley scales of infant development*. San Antonio, TX: The Psychological Corp.

Beckwith, L. (1988). Intervention with disadvantaged parents of sick preterm infants. *Psychiatry, 51*, 242–247.

Birch, H., & Gussow, G. D. (1970). *Disadvantaged children*. New York: Grune & Stratton.

Blatt, S. D., Saletsky, R. D., Meguid, V., Church, C. C., O'Hara, M. T., Haller–Peck, S. M., & Anderson, J. M. (1997). A comprehensive, multidisciplinary approach to providing health care for children in out-of-home care. *Child Welfare, 76*, 331–347.

Bzoch, K. R., & League, R. (1991). *Receptive-expressive emergent language test* (2nd ed.). Austin, TX: Pro-Ed.

Carnegie Corporation of New York. (1994). *Starting points: Meeting the needs of our youngest children*. New York: Author.

Chernoff, R., Combs-Orne, T., Risley-Curtiss, C., & Heisler, A. (1994). Assessing the health status of children entering foster care. *Pediatrics, 93*, 594-601.

Davis, S., & Caruso, M. A. (1999). Insuring family and community life for infants who are medically fragile: A multidisciplinary approach to early intervention and family support. In J. Silver, B. Amster, & T. Haecker (Eds.), *Young children and foster care: A guide for professionals*. Baltimore: Paul H. Brookes Publishing Co.

Drotar, D., Malone, C. A., & Negray, J. (1980). Intellectual assessment of young children with environmentally based failure to thrive. *Child Abuse & Neglect, 4*, 23–31.

Dunst, C. J. (1993). Implications of risk and opportunity factors for assessment and intervention practices. *Topics in Early Childhood Special Education, 13*, 143–153.

Folio, M. R., & Fewell, R. (1983). *The Peabody developmental motor scales and activity cards*. Hingham, MA: Teaching Resources Corp.

Frank, G. (1980). Treatment needs of children in foster care. *American Journal of Orthopsychiatry, 50*, 256–263.

Halfon, N., Berkowitz, G., & Klee, L. (1992). Mental health service utilization by children in foster care in California. *Pediatrics, 89*, 1238–1244.

Halfon, N., & Klee, L. (1987). Health services for California's foster children: Current practices and policy recommendations. *Pediatrics, 80*, 183–191.

Halfon, N., & Klee, L. (1991). Health and development services for children with multiple needs: The child in foster care. *Yale Law and Policy Review, 9*, 71–96.

Halfon, N., Mendonca, A., & Berkowitz, G. (1995). Health status of children in foster care. *Archives of Pediatric and Adolescent Medicine, 149*, 386–392.

Hochstadt, N. J., Jaudes, P. K., Zimo, D. A., & Schachter, J. (1987). The medical and psychosocial needs of children entering foster care. *Child Abuse & Neglect, 11*, 53–62.

Hornblower, M. (1995, December 11). Fixing the system. *Time, 146*(24), 44–45.

Horowitz, S. M., Simms, M. D., & Farrington, R. (1994). Impact of developmental problems on young children's exits from foster care. *Developmental and Behavioral Pediatrics, 15*, 105–110.

Infant Health and Development Program. (1990). Enhancing the outcomes of low–birth-weight, premature infants: A multisite, randomized trial. *Journal of the American Medical Association, 263*, 3035–3042.

Klee, L., & Kronstadt, D. (1999). Linking services, research and policy for children in foster care: Lessons learned. In J. Silver, B. Amster, & T. Haecker (Eds.), *Young children and foster care: A guide for professionals*. Baltimore: Paul H. Brookes Publishing Co.

Kutzler, P. (1998). *Profiles of children 2.5 years or younger at time of placement placed initially in calendar years 1995 and 1996.* Unpublished raw data from the Family and Child Tracking System, Philadelphia Department of Human Services.

Moffat, M. E. K., Peddie, M., Stulginskas, J., Pless, I. B., & Steinmetz, N. (1985). Health care delivery to foster children: A study. *Health and Social Work, 10,* 129–137.

Peckham, V. C. (1999). Family School: Twenty years as an innovative model demonstration project. In J. Silver, B. Amster, & T. Haecker (Eds.), *Young children and foster care: A guide for professionals.* Baltimore: Paul H. Brookes Publishing Co.

Sameroff, A. J. (1993). Models of development and developmental risk. In C. H. Zeanah (Ed.), *Handbook of infant mental health* (pp. 3–13). New York: Guilford Press.

Sameroff, A., & Chandler, M. J. (1975). Reproductive risk and the continuum of caretaking casualty. In F. D. Horowitz, M. Hetherington, S. Scarr–Salapatek, & G. Siegel (Eds.), *Review of child development research (vol.4)* (pp. 187–244). Chicago: University of Chicago Press.

Schor, E. L. (1982). The foster care system and health status of foster children. *Pediatrics, 69,* 521–528.

Schorr, L. B. (1997). *Common purpose: Strengthening families and neighborhoods to rebuild America.* NY: Doubleday.

Shonkoff, J., & Hauser-Cram, P. (1987). Early identification for disabled infants and their families: A quantitative analysis. *Pediatrics, 80,* 650–658.

Sigman, M., & Parmelee, A. H. (1979). Longitudinal evaluation of the preterm infant. In T. M. Field, A. M. Sostek, S. Goldberg, & H. H. Shuman (Eds.), *Infants born at risk* (pp. 193–219). New York: Spectrum.

Simms, M. (1989). The foster care clinic: A community program to identify treatment needs of children in foster care. *Developmental and Behavioral Pediatrics, 10,* 121–128.

Simms, M. D., & Halfon, N. (1994). The health care needs of children in foster care: A research agenda. *Child Welfare, 73,* 505–524.

Smolowe, J. (1995, December 11). Making the tough calls. *Time, 146*(24), 40–44.

Spiker, D., & Silver, J. (1999). Early intervention for infants and preschoolers in foster care. In J. Silver, B. Amster, & T. Haecker (Eds.), *Young children and foster care: A guide for professionals.* Baltimore: Paul H. Brookes Publishing Co.

Spitz, R. (1945). Hospitalism: An inquiry into the genesis of psychiatric conditions in early childhood. In A. Freud, W. Hoffer, E. Glover, P. Greenacre, H. Hartman, E. B. Jackson, E. Kris, L. S. Kubie, B. Lewin, & M. C. Putnam (Eds.), *Psychoanalytic study of the child (vol. 1)* (pp. 52–74). New York: International University Press.

Spitz, R. (1946). Hospitalism: A follow-up report on investigation described in Volume I, 1945. In A. Freud, W. Hoffer, E. Glover, P. Greenacre, H. Hartman, E. B. Jackson, E. Kris, L. S. Kubie, B. Lewin, & M. C. Putnam (Eds.), *Psychoanalytic study of the child (vol. 2)* (pp. 113–117). New York: International University Press.

Takayama, J. I., Bergman, A. B., & Connell, F. A. (1994). Children in foster care in the state of Washington: Health care utilization and expenditures. *Journal of the American Medical Association, 271*, 1850–1855.

Teti, D. M., & Gibbs, E. D. (1990). Infant assessment: Historical antecedents and contemporary issues. In E. D. Gibbs & D. M. Teti (Eds.), *Interdisciplinary assessment of infants: A guide for early intervention professionals* (pp. 3–13). Baltimore: Paul H. Brookes Publishing Co.

U. S. General Accounting Office. (1995). *Foster care: Health needs of many young children are unknown and unmet.* Washington, DC: Author (GAO/HEHS–95–114).

Wulczyn, F., & Goerge, R. (1992). Foster care in New York and Illinois: The challenge of rapid change. *Social Service Review, 66*, 278–294.

Zimmerman, I. L., Steiner, V. G., & Pond, R. E. (1992). *Preschool language scale (3rd ed.).* San Antonio, TX: The Psychological Corporation; Harcourt & Brace & Co.

Delivering Health and Mental Health Care Services to Children in Family Foster Care after

9 Welfare and Health Care Reform

Mark D. Simms, Madelyn Freundlich, Ellen S. Battistelli, and Neal D. Kaufman

As the 20th century draws to a close, fundamental changes in the organization, financing, and delivery of health care and welfare services, principally directed at poor families, are likely to result in an increased number of children entering out-of-home care. These children typically have significant physical, mental health, and developmental problems. Whether the quality of health care services they receive will improve as a result of health care reform efforts and new approaches to service delivery remains to be seen. This article addresses some of the major changes wrought by welfare and health care reform and describes the essential features of a health care system that can meet the special needs of children in care.

Mark D. Simms, M.D., M.P.H., is Associate Professor of Pediatrics, Department of Pediatrics, Medical College of Wisconsin, Milwaukee, WI. Madelyn Freundlich, J.D., M.S.W., M.P.H., is Executive Director, The Evan B. Donaldson Adoption Institute, New York, NY. Ellen S. Battistelli, B.A., is Senior Policy Analyst, Child Welfare League

Nearly 500,000 children are in the out-of-home care system, despite concerted federal and state efforts to prevent out-of-home placement over the past two decades [National Committee to Prevent Child Abuse 1997; Petit & Curtis 1997]. Although these children have high rates of health and mental health problems, they have difficulty accessing timely and appropriate health care services. Over a decade ago, the Child Welfare League of America (CWLA), in consultation with the American Academy of Pediatrics (AAP), published *Standards for Health Care Services for Children in Out-of-Home Care* to serve as a blueprint for developing effective service delivery structures for children in out-of-home care [Child Welfare League of America 1987]. More recently, the American Academy of Pediatrics Committee on Early Childhood, Adoption and Dependent Care issued a statement to pediatricians entitled *Health Care of Children in Foster Care* [American Academy of Pediatrics 1994]. Unfortunately, for a variety of reasons, these standards and guidelines have generally not been implemented.

As America enters the next century, the organization, financing, and delivery of health care and welfare services to the poor are undergoing fundamental changes. At the federal level, social support programs, such as Aid for Families with Dependent Children (AFDC), are being restructured, and responsibility for the cost and delivery of basic services is being shifted to state governments. The creation of the Temporary Assistance for Needy Families (TANF) program and changes in the Supplemental Security Income (SSI) program for children with disabilities, as brought about by the Personal Responsibility and Work Opportunity Act of 1996 [P.L. 104-193], reflect a new policy environment [Green & Waters 1997]. In the area of health care, state governments are working hard to transfer the financial risk and responsibility for delivering services under Medicaid to private,

of America, Washington, DC. Neal D. Kaufman, M.D., M.P.H., is Professor of Pediatrics and Public Health, UCLA School of Medicine and Public Health, Department of Pediatrics, Cedars-Sinai Medical Center, Los Angeles, CA.

managed care organizations (MCOs) [Henry J. Kaiser Family Foundation 1996]. To eliminate the ineffectiveness and limit escalating costs of these programs, policymakers are turning to "new approaches" that have no proven record of success with their respective "target" populations [Battistelli 1996]. Thus, the impact that welfare reform and health care reform efforts may have on children who enter the out-of-home care system in the next century is not clear.

This article focuses on the health care status and needs of children in family foster care and examines how this group of vulnerable children has been affected by welfare reform, the growth in managed care, and other health care reform efforts over the past several years. It examines the significant role that Medicaid has played in meeting the health care needs of children in care and considers the impact of Medicaid managed care and other factors related to access on the ability of child welfare systems to meet the health care needs of children in the future. It concludes with recommendations that address the attributes of a health care system that must be in place so that children in out-of-home care will receive the critical physical, mental health, and developmental services they need, and their biological and adoptive families will have access to health care services on an ongoing basis.

Welfare Reform

Recent changes in family policy, particularly with regard to poor children and families, likely mean that more poor children will enter out-of-home care over the next decade and that these children will enter care with significant health problems. The shrinking of the "safety net" (formerly represented by the AFDC and SSI programs) for families and the passage of the Personal Responsibility and Work Opportunity Reconciliation Act of 1996 (P.L. 104-193), popularly known as the "welfare reform" act, may have a powerful impact on the level of child poverty in the future, and consequently, on the health care status of children in general and on children who enter out-of-home care, in particular. Welfare reform ended the previously guaranteed benefits for poor families under the AFDC program (two-thirds of whose recipients were poor children); significantly reduced the Food Stamp program (with reductions primarily affecting families with children); and made substantial changes in the SSI program (with loss of benefits for thousands of children with mental health and emotional disorders and multiple impairments) [Waxman & Alker 1996; Children's Defense Fund 1996; National Health Law Program 1996].

Reports from the field suggest that reductions in welfare, Food Stamps, and disability benefits are creating significant stresses on families that may further intensify as the full impact of welfare reform is realized. With the discretion given to them under welfare reform for the implementation of the new TANF program, many states are adopting stricter work requirements and shorter time limits than those set as minimum standards in the law [Pear 1997a]. Early reports suggest that those who have lost benefits because of these new policies are not readily finding employment. A survey conducted by the New York State Office of Temporary and Disability Assistance, for example, found that less than one-third of the people who lost benefits in New York State between July 1996 and March 1997 had secured full or part-time jobs [Hernandez 1998]. Seventy percent of the reductions in Food Stamps have impacted families with children [Children's Defense Fund 1996], more than a hundred thousand children have been denied SSI benefits, some erroneously; and a substantial percentage of children denied SSI have also lost their Medicaid coverage [Pear 1997b; Waxman & Alker 1996]. The cumulative impact of these policy and program changes, because of their effects on families' abilities to support their children, is likely to be increasing numbers of children entering out-of-home care, most of whom will be poor and whose health will be significantly compromised.

Health Care Reform

Since 1965, the Medicaid program has provided health care benefits for millions of poor children and families [National Health Law Program 1996]. One key provision of this program—the Early Periodic Screening, Diagnosis, and Treatment (EPSDT) program—attempts to ensure that enrolled children receive a wide range of preventive, diagnostic, and therapeutic services. Compliance with these requirements, however has generally been poor. Despite the rapid rise in total expenditures for Medicaid generally, physician and hospital payment schedules have failed to keep pace with the rising cost of providing health care services. As a result, the number of physicians who are willing to treat Medicaid recipients has declined nationwide [Yudkowsky et al. 1990]. Thus, the very program that enables poor children to receive health care services acts as a significant obstacle, limiting their access to the best or most appropriate medical care available.

Despite Medicaid's limitations, there is no question that it remains the single most important source of care for children in out-of-home placement and for troubled families. Most states view Medicaid, and its EPSDT program for children, as a costly federal mandate. The states want increased flexibility over implementation of the Medicaid program and both the states and Congress seek reductions in Medicaid spending. Relaxing the federal requirements or decreasing funding for this program, however, could undermine the availability of needed medical services even further.

To limit the financial burden associated with Medicaid, to improve access to care, and to provide a higher quality of services, state governments are turning to private, managed care organizations (MCOs) and enrolling Medicaid-eligible families in managed care programs. In contrast to the "traditional" fee-for-service (FFS) insurance system, in which insurers pass excess costs for services onto the enrollees, employers, or government payors through higher premium rates, MCOs assume the full financial "risk" for providing sufficient services to their enrollees by accepting a fixed sum of money for each person covered. In turn, they distribute this risk among the components of their plan, including physicians, hospitals, pharmacies, etc. Without doubt, the major attraction of the managed care approach is its potential to limit or reduce overall health care costs. The financial pressures to contain the cost of care provides powerful incentives to identify and provide effective services in the most efficient manner. MCOs, however, walk a thin line between providing too many "unnecessary" services that drain limited dollars or providing too few "necessary" services that may result in the progression of problems and ultimately, more expensive care. Thus, the managed care paradigm relies heavily on the principle of primary, preventive care as the most cost-effective approach. Accordingly, patients in these plans are encouraged to obtain prevention-oriented services such as screening examinations to detect treatable conditions as early as possible. Medical treatments, in turn, are subjected to careful scrutiny regarding their effectiveness and cost, and managed care plans are strongly vested in tracking and monitoring the quantity and quality of care members receive. Many plans require preauthorization before consultations and tests are approved, and employ patient care managers to oversee how members move through their systems. The increased regulation of services under managed care makes it less likely that patients will "fall through the cracks."

The Health Problems of Children in Out-of-Home Care

Children entering care have unusually poor health compared with their peers from similar social and ethnic backgrounds who live at home [Simms 1991]. Many of these children have suffered physical injuries as a result of abuse, and most have experienced some form of physical and/or emotional neglect prior to placement. Not unexpectedly, chronic medical conditions and mental health disorders are extremely common, as are birth defects and physical growth disorders [Hochstadt et al. 1987; Simms 1989; Chernoff et al. 1994; Halfon et al. 1995; Rosenfeld et al. 1997].

Several studies have examined the costs of providing health and mental health care services to this population. In 1992, Halfon et al. found that the major expense category for children in out-of-home care involved hospitalization, particularly for perinatal problems, mental health disorders, and infections [Halfon et al. 1992a, 1992b]. Overall length of stay for all hospitalizations was nearly twice as long for children in out-of-home care (10.9 days vs. 6.0 days), and utilization of outpatient mental health care services was strikingly increased. Although children in out-of-home care comprised only 4% of the population of children covered by MediCal in 1988, they received 55% of all visits to psychologists and 45% of all visits to psychiatrists paid by the program.

In 1990, Takayama compared the health care costs of children in out-of-home care to other children receiving AFDC in Washington state [Takayama et al. 1994]. The annual mean health care cost for a child in care was nearly sixfold greater than that for a child not in care ($3,075 vs. $543). Children in care also had significantly greater utilization of mental health care services (25% vs. 7%); supportive care from visiting nurses, physical therapists, etc. (13% vs. 1%); and hospitalization (10% vs. 5%). When the authors stratified the population according to annual amount of health care cost, they found children in care overrepresented in each group. It should be noted that a small group of children (8% of the total) had annual expenses that exceeded $10,000. These children, who largely suffered from mental health, neurological, or congenital anomalies, consumed 63% of all the dollars spent on health care for children in out-of-home care.

Obstacles to the Delivery of Health Care Services

Children in out-of-home care have a wide range of health care needs. Yet, despite their high rates of medical and mental health problems, most children in care do not receive the health care services they need [U.S. General Accounting Office 1995]. As a result, needed health care services are often delayed or not provided. A 1995 study by the U.S. General Accounting Office evaluated the health care received by nearly 23,000 children in out-of-home care under the age of 3 in Los Angeles, New York City, and Philadelphia, and found that many important health-related needs remained unmet [U.S. General Accounting Office 1995]. Furthermore, the study concluded that current state and federal efforts do not ensure that these children receive appropriate health care services. Indeed, the scope of the health care services provided to children in out-of-home care is often not comprehensive, nor is it matched to each child's unique circumstances. For example, as specified in the Child Welfare League of America's *Standards* and in the American Academy of Pediatrics guidelines, each child entering out-of-home care should have access to a range of services, including the collection of evidence that abuse and/or neglect has occurred; an assessment for any significant urgent health care needs or restrictions on the type of placement the children will experience; an assessment of their health, dental, developmental, and mental health care needs; the development of a plan to address their identified needs; and case management and care coordination services.

Practical experience suggests that a variety of factors act as true barriers to care for these children. For example, most public and private agencies caring for children in out-of-home care have no formal policies or arrangements to provide health care services, relying instead on local physicians and health care clinics funded by Medicaid. Information about children's utilization of health care services and their status prior to placement is often hard to obtain—in part because the children have had erratic contact with a number of different health care providers prior to placement and social workers are not always able to review the child's health history in detail with the biological parents at the time children are taken into care. Once in family foster care, much of the responsibility for obtaining health care services is placed on foster parents, who often have been given little or no training in health care issues or in accessing the health care system [Battistelli 1997]. For their part, social workers frequently lack information about the type or content of health care services that children in family foster care receive and are unable to effectively oversee the amount or quality of the care delivered. As a result, foster parents are left alone to sort out the health problems of the children in their care and to maneuver in an unwieldy health care system. Compounding this situation is the fact that many of the children have complex health problems and require care from a variety of medical specialists.

The systems providing care to these children are often inadequate and not coordinated by the responsible child welfare agency or the courts, nor is the care integrated among the various providers of care. The inability to transfer information between providers and agencies, and the lack of collection of health status data on the children, leads to further fragmentation and poor outcomes. Unfortunately, there have been a number of "high profile" media cases involving children in family foster care who were harmed because critical health information was not known or communicated to the adults who were caring for them. This diffusion of responsibility can also result in the delay or denial of care when issues of proper authority are not explicitly resolved.

Nearly three-quarters of children experience more than one family foster home placement during their time in the out-of-home care system. These changes in residences and caregivers often disrupt the fragile care networks that are established, since the children usually change their health care providers as well. Similarly, changes in social workers are exceedingly common and, as a result, key aspects in the planning and coordination of efforts on the child's behalf may be lost. Finally, the benefit package provided to the children is seldom comprehensive, especially in the area of mental health care services. Despite the federal guarantee of benefits for low-income children under Medicaid, state compliance has often been incomplete, particularly in the implementation of such well-designed benefits as EPSDT. Because health care systems are complex and involve the participation of multiple providers and agencies, the lack of independent evaluation of the overall effectiveness of the health care provided to children in out-of-home care hinders rational policymaking and systems development.

Implications for Permanency Planning

These obstacles to health care delivery have profound implications both for the health and well-being of children and for effective permanency planning for children in out-of-home care. The entry of children into care has been consistently associated with poverty; exit from care is associated with the provision of services to families and children to ensure that families can effectively resume responsibility for meeting their children's needs [Lindsey 1994; Pelton 1989]. Analyses of length of time in out-of-home care suggest that, even with AFDC supports in place, children have remained in care for extended periods of time [Chapin Hall Center for Children 1994]. As families lose TANF benefits, Medicaid coverage, and Food Stamps, and children lose the SSI benefits that made it possible for them to obtain essential health care and developmental services, reunification may be more difficult to achieve. Even when reunification is possible, even longer periods of time to accomplish it may be required than were previously the case. Families are likely to face new challenges in regaining custody of their children, and the child welfare system may find it difficult to ensure that biological families can obtain health care and developmental services when their children return to them.

The State Children's Health Insurance Program (established in 1997 to expand health care access for poor children and now Title XXI of the Social Security Act [P.L. 105-33]) provides no guarantee that all children will receive continuous, comprehensive health care. At the same time, the Adoption and Safe Families Act of 1997 (P.L. 105-89) may affect the permanency outcomes for many poor children and their families. On the one hand, the law targets funds from Title IV-B (now retitled the Promoting Safe and Stable Families Program) for time-limited reunification services such as counseling, substance abuse treatment, mental health services, and assistance for domestic violence—services that could potentially promote reunification through intensive efforts. On the other hand, the act's mandates will prompt states to consider termination of parental rights more quickly and may result in freeing for adoption greater numbers of children who entered out-of-home care because of poverty-based factors.

As a consequence, the number of children in out-of-home care who will require adoption planning and services may increase. These children, like the majority of children in family foster care, will have medical and mental health care problems and will need ongoing health care services. The percentage of children in out-of-home care with special needs who are awaiting adoptive placements has been increasing steadily. National data shows that the percentage of these children rose from 47% in FY 1984 to almost 72% in 1990 [Tatara 1993]. More recent state-based data demonstrate that even larger percentages of waiting children in out-of-home care have special needs: 84% of the children adopted in New York State during 1992-93 had special needs (Avery & Mont 1994) and 95% of the children placed for adoption in California during 1993-94 had one or more physical or emotional problems [California Department of Social Services 1995]. Many of these children with special needs have physical, emotional, and mental disabilities [Tatara 1993]. It is reasonable to anticipate that the vast majority of children entering care in the future who cannot be reunited with their biological families will likewise have significant health care problems that will require medical and mental health care services during their stays in family foster care and after their adoption.

Welfare reform, however, will create greater complexity in

qualifying these "special needs" children for adoption assistance, as it links Title IV-E eligibility to eligibility for the former AFDC programs, as those eligibility rules existed on June 1, 1995. As a result, eligibility for Title IV-E adoption assistance and Medicaid is linked with eligibility for a program that no longer exists (AFDC) and is based on a 1995 standard of poverty that will become less appropriate as an indicator of poverty with the passage of time. Efforts to "delink" Title IV-E adoption assistance from AFDC were unsuccessful in 1997, although the Adoption and Safe Families Act did expand health care coverage to non-Title IV-E eligible children with special health care needs. This may provide many children who are unable to qualify for Title IV-E adoption assistance (and the Medicaid coverage it carries) with health care coverage that, according to the new law, must be equivalent to the benefits offered by Medicaid. Nonetheless, the complexity associated with the current interface of welfare reform, Title IV-E adoption assistance, and the health care mandates of the Adoption and Safe Families Act raises many questions about the extent to which the child welfare system will be able to effectively meet the health care and permanency needs of children in out-of-home care.

Managed Health Care for Children in Out-of-Home Care

Considering the unique health care needs of children in family foster care, and the obstacles they experience in accessing services, managed health care programs may offer several distinct advantages and potential opportunities to improve the care these children receive and to promote effective permanency planning. The emphasis that MCOs usually place on primary care and early identification of problems may increase the likelihood that all children entering out-of-home care receive timely health and mental health evaluations. The coordinated network of health care providers and patient care managers, and the information systems that MCOs employ to monitor service delivery, may also help to ensure that children have access to a full range of appropriate services and that their problems are properly attended to, even if the child welfare agency's staff is not able to adequately oversee the health care of its clients. Similarly, even if children change family foster homes or social workers, by remaining enrolled in the same managed health care plan, continuity of care and health information may be assured.

Managed care for children in family foster care, however, is not without significant potential problems. To the extent that managed care has been successful, its benefits have largely flowed to individuals in good health, not those with special health care needs. Indeed, managed care organizations are often referred to as health maintenance organizations (HMOs). Yet, as noted previously, children in out-of-home care are generally in poor health and many require care for chronic illnesses by specialists and a wide range of habilitative and rehabilitative services. Major concerns about managed care include the restricted access to specialists for individuals with chronic diseases, particularly psychological and developmental disorders, and the huge profits that are reported by MCOs. Critics of managed care accuse MCOs of not applying their cost savings toward increasing the range of services or lowering enrollment fees. Instead, investors in MCOs react negatively when too much of the plan's funds are paid out in health care services (the so-called "medical-loss ratio").

For children in family foster care, the actual cost of delivering the full range of appropriate health and mental health care services may be much higher than current estimates would suggest. The studies by Halfon and Takayama looked at actual costs in systems that did not specifically screen and refer children with problems; both authors suggested that their data probably underestimated the level of true need [Halfon et al. 1992a, 1992b]. Takayama et al. 1994]. If the children were to receive early evaluations and appropriate care for their conditions, however, as recommended by CWLA and AAP, the total costs might actually decline over the long run. This might be particularly true if savings resulting from improved child and family health in other areas, such as child welfare, juvenile justice, and education, are taken into consideration. Until additional data are available on how children in family foster care fare in managed care, child welfare agencies and MCOs should not expect an immediate savings in overall health and mental health care costs by shifting this population out of fee-for-service programs and into managed care. Child welfare agencies should also exercise caution when choosing or approving a managed care benefits "package" unless it guarantees sufficient access to an extensive array of pediatric subspecialists, mental health care services, and habilitative services, and complies with the provisions of CWLA's and AAP's standards for health care for this population.

Also of concern is the fact that managed care for children in out-of-home care may not be readily transferable when children return to their biological families or are placed with adoptive families. Some level of continuity of care may be assured by managed care for children in out-of-home care, but significant issues exist concerning continuing access to quality care after children are reunited with their biological families or adopted. Eligibility issues, particularly through Medicaid, and limitations on geographic scope of coverage may mean that the benefits achieved for a child through managed health care during the child's family foster care stay will not be sustained after the child leaves care. Consideration of continuity of care and maintenance of health care benefits after care is critical.

Recommendations

Regardless of the financing mechanisms or organizational structures that are put into place, any system of health care for children in foster care should have the following attributes:

- comprehensive services with clearly stated standards of care (e.g., CWLA and/or AAP);

- portable benefits while the child remains in out-of-home care;
- presumptive eligibility for Medicaid upon removal of the child from the home, regardless of the biological parent's eligibility status;
- continuous eligibility for a minimum of 12 months and—in an effort to ensure that treatment and rehabilitative services can continue after placement—extension of eligibility for another 12 months after the child has left the out-of-home care system;
- social service case coordination and case management services;
- incentives to encourage participation by health care providers; and
- a local and state governance system that clearly identifies who is responsible for the implementation and enforcement of the standards, procedures, and guidelines.

The system must work in urban and rural areas with and without managed care plans and with or without a large supply of primary or specialty providers. A statewide data system should also be established.

Conclusions

Children in out-of-home care are extremely vulnerable, with unusually poor health when compared to their peers who live at home. Recent changes in the nation's family policies are likely to lead to large numbers of children entering out-of-home care and even greater risks to the health and well-being of these children. The shift from fee-for-service to managed care offers the potential to improve the organization, financing, and delivery of health care services to children in the out-of-home care system, and managed care's emphasis on primary and preventive care and the coordination of services may help to overcome some of the greatest obstacles to health care for this population. Care must be taken, however, to ensure that sufficient access is provided to the services that this special group of children require.

Society will be hard pressed to cure the ills of child welfare without improving the nation's health care system. Appropriate health insurance can prevent children and families from needing assistance by the child welfare system. Accessible, affordable, quality health and mental health care services can address problems that, left untreated, explode into devastating family and community problems. Similarly, the availability of health care services is critical to solving family problems and reuniting children with their parents. As America heads into a new century, these most vulnerable children must not be allowed to pass from a poor system into a worse one.◆

References

American Academy of Pediatrics, Committee on Early Childhood, Adoption and Dependent Care. (1994). Health care of children in foster care. *Pediatrics, 93*, 335-338.

Avery, R. J., & Mont, D. M. (1994). *Special needs adoption in New York State: Final report on adoptive parent survey. Final report to the United States Department of Health and Human Services.* Ithaca, NY: Cornell University.

Battistelli, E. S. (1996). *Making managed health care work for kids in foster care.* Washington, DC: CWLA Press.

Battistelli, E. S. (1997). *Managed health care guide for caseworkers and foster parents.* Washington, DC: CWLA Press.

California Department of Social Services. (1995). *A characteristics publication describing the characteristics of children, birth parents, and adoptive parents involved in agency adoptions in California from July 1993 through June 1994.* Sacramento, CA: California Department of Social Services, Information Services Bureau.

Chapin Hall Center for Children at the University of Chicago. (1994). *An update from the multistate foster care data archive: Foster care dynamics 1983-1993—California, Illinois, Michigan, New York and Texas.* Chicago: University of Chicago, Chapin Hall Center for Children.

Chernoff, R., Combs-Orme, T., Risley-Curtiss, C., & Heisler, A. (1994). Assessing the health status of children entering foster care. *Pediatrics, 93*, 594-601.

Child Welfare League of America. (1988). *Standards for health care services for children in out-of-home care.* Washington, DC: Author.

Children's Defense Fund. (1996, October 24). Summary of new welfare law. [Online]. Available at http://www.tmn.com/dcf/welfarelaw.html.

Green, R., & Waters, S. (1997). *The impact of welfare reform on child welfare financing.* Series A, No. 4-16. Washington, DC: The Urban Institute.

Halfon, N., Berkowitz, G., & Klee, L. (1992a). Children in foster care in California: An examination of Medicaid reimbursed health services utilization. *Pediatrics, 89*, 1230-1237.

Halfon, N., Berkowitz, G., & Klee, L. (1992b). Mental health service utilization by children in foster care in California. *Pediatrics, 89*, 1238-1244.

Halfon, N. G., Mendonca, A., & Berkowitz, G. (1995). Health status of children in foster care: The experience of the Center for the Vulnerable Child. *Archives of Pediatrics and Adolescent Medicine, 149*, 386-392.

Henry J. Kaiser Family Foundation. (1996). *Medicaid facts: Medicaid and managed care.* Washington, DC: The Kaiser Commission on the Future of Medicaid.

Hernandez, R. (1998, March 23). People not going from welfare into jobs, New York survey says. *The New York Times*, p. A1.

Hochstadt, N. J., Jaudes, P. K., Zimo, D. A., & Schachter, J. (1987). The medical and psychosocial needs of children entering foster care. *Child Abuse and Neglect, 11*, 53-62.

Lindsey, D. (1994). *The welfare of children.* New York: Oxford University Press.

National Committee to Prevent Child Abuse. (1997). *Current trends in child abuse reporting and fatalities: The results of the 1996 annual 50-state survey.* Chicago: Author.

National Health Law Program, National Center for Youth Law, & National Senior Citizen's Law Center. (1996). An analysis of the new welfare law and its effects on Medicaid recipients. *Special Edition Newsletter.*

Pear, R. (1997a, February 23). Rewards and penalties vary in states' welfare programs. *The New York Times*, p. A12.

Pear, R. (1997b, November 16). Disabled youths are wrongly cut from aid program. *The New York Times*, pp. A1, A20.

Pelton, L. H. (1989). *For reasons of poverty*. New York: Praeger.

Petit, M. R., & Curtis, P. A. (1997). *Child abuse and neglect: A look at the states—The 1997 CWLA stat book*. Washington, DC: CWLA Press.

Rosenfeld, A. A., Pilowsky, D. J., Fine, P., Thorpe, M., Fein, E., Simms, M. D., Halfon, N., Irwin, M., Alfaro, J., Saletsky, R., & Nickman, S. (1997). Foster care: An update. *Journal of the American Academy of Child and Adolescent Psychiatry, 36*, 448-457.

Simms, M. D. (1989). The foster care clinic: A community program to identify treatment needs of children in foster care. *Journal of Developmental and Behavioral Pediatrics, 10*, 121-128.

Simms, M. D. (1991). Foster children and the foster care system, Part II: Impact on the child. *Current Problems in Pediatrics, 21*, 345-370.

Takayama, J. I., Bergman, A. B., & Connell, F. A. (1994). Children in foster care in the state of Washington: Health care utilization and expenditures. *Journal of the American Medical Association, 271*, 1850-1855.

Tatara, T. (1993). *Voluntary cooperative information system (VCIS), Characteristics of children in substitute and adoptive care [Based on FY 82 through FY 90 data]*. Washington, DC: American Public Welfare Association.

U.S. General Accounting Office. (1995). *Health needs of many young children are unknown and unmet* (GAO/HEHS-95-114). Washington, DC: U.S. General Accounting Office.

Waxman, J., & Alker, J. (1996, August 19). The impact of federal welfare reform on Medicaid. [Online]. Available at http://www.handsnet.org/medicaid/impact.htm.

Yudkowsky, B. K., Cartland, J. D., & Flint, S. S. (1990). Pediatrician participation in Medicaid: 1978-1989. *Pediatrics, 85*, 567-577.

The Impact of Drug-Exposed
10 Children on Family Foster Care

Theresa McNichol

To determine whether infants exposed to drugs during gestation present special challenges in family foster care, data on 204 infants were reviewed. Developmental functioning, health and caregiving needs, visits by biological parents, and case dispositions were compared across drug-exposure groups. Infants with verified drug exposure presented with significantly more health and caregiving needs, had fewer biological parent visits, and were more frequently placed with relatives after family foster care. Findings are discussed in terms of their impact on family foster care in the next century.

Theresa McNichol, Ph.D., is Clinical and Research Psychologist, Children's Bureau of Southern California, Los Angeles, CA.

Following the "epidemic" of cocaine use during the last two decades, concerns have arisen about the potential problems infants and children might encounter following exposure to cocaine (and other illegal drugs) during gestation. One study placed the incidence of newborns exposed to illegal drugs at 11% of live births, resulting in an estimated 375,000 affected infants born each year [Chasnoff et al. 1990]. Studies of these infants show that they are smaller in weight and head size, and that they are more irritable and difficult to comfort than infants not exposed to illegal drugs [Hurt et al. 1995; Phillips et al. 1996]. A study that examined 3-year-old children who were exposed to illegal drugs during gestation did not find significant differences in cognitive development compared to children not exposed, but did find that the children exposed to drugs had a lower level of perseverance for completing tasks [Azuma & Chasnoff 1993]. Other research suggests that gestational exposure to illegal drugs may not influence overall cognitive development, but rather, negatively impact the mechanisms involved in the regulation of emotional states and attention to complex learning tasks [Vogel 1997].

This study begins the search for answers to the many questions about the later development of children exposed to illegal drugs during gestation by examining the needs and development of drug-exposed infants who were subsequently placed in care.

Purpose

The study reported here sought to determine how many infants exposed to drugs during gestation were placed from 1990 through 1997 in a large, nonprofit, metropolitan, out-of-home care agency, and whether the developmental functioning and presentation of health and caregiving needs of these infants differed from those of infants not exposed to drugs who were also placed by the agency. The involvement of the biological parents in terms of frequency of visits and the disposition of the children after leaving the agency were also examined.

Method and Demographic Characteristics

To answer these questions, the case experiences of 204 infants placed for family foster care with an agency that serves two, large, southern California counties (the Children's Bureau of Southern California) were analyzed. The group studied included all infants who were currently in placement (76 cases, or 37% of the sample), or who had been discharged (128 cases, or 63% of the sample) as of December 31, 1997. The infants included in the study were placed at an age ranging from shortly after birth to 15 months.

The study population comprised 109 males (53.4%) and 95 females (46.6%). These children were of African American (n = 92, 45.1%), Latino (n = 50, 24.5%), Caucasian (n = 58, 28.4%), part American Indian (n = 3, 1.5%), or part Asian (n = 1, .5%) heritage.

Data were collected by a researcher reviewing the closed cases, and by the case manager (social worker) and researcher recording data from current or open cases. Uniform file documents that include demographic, referral, health needs, visiting, and disposition information were searched. Scores indicating the level of cognitive and motor functioning were taken from psychological assessment reports, which utilized standardized, individually administered tests (e.g., the Bayley Scales of Infant Development).

Of the 204 infants studied, the stated reason for placement was as follows: 44.1% (90) due to being born "drug exposed" and parental custody being assessed as unsafe; 15.7% (32) due to neglect; 9.8% (20) due to mental disability of the biological mother; 8.3% (17) due to physical abuse of the child or siblings; 5.9% (12) because the mother was in jail or prison; 5.4% (11) due to problems surrounding parental substance abuse; 5.4% (11) due to abandonment; 2% (4) due to domestic violence; 2% (4) for other reasons; and, 1.5% (3) due to sexual abuse of the child or siblings. It is interesting to note that the number of infants with verified drug exposure (126) is larger than the number born "drug exposed"; some of these infants were taken into care for nondrug-related problems such as neglect, abuse, or abandonment.

Exposure of the infant to illegal drugs during gestation was verified in 61.7% of the 204 cases through toxicology tests during pregnancy or at the time of birth (usually urine toxicology of mother and/or child) or by acknowledgment by the biological mother; these cases comprise Group 1 (n = 126). Another 16.7% of the infants came from families involved in substance abuse where there was "some suspicion" of drug exposure during gestation; these cases comprise Group 2 (n = 34). Finally, 21.6% of the infants were believed to have no exposure to illegal drugs during gestation; these cases comprise Group 3 cases (n = 44). Alcohol exposure during gestation, noted in documentation to be present in some cases, and known to have deleterious effects on the fetus, could not be accurately assessed from a review of the records because of inconsistent reporting [Mattson et al. 1998].

Findings

Drug Identification

In cases in which the illegal drug used by the mother during pregnancy was identified (116), the drug was cocaine 71% of the time, amphetamines 20% of the time, heroin 5% of the time, and marijuana 3% of the time. For cases where a second drug was identified (33), the drug was marijuana 52% of the time, amphetamines 15% of the time, heroin or PCP 12% of the time, cocaine 6% of the time, and methadone 3% of the time.

Age at Placement

Infants in Group 1 were placed at an earlier age, a mean age of 3.8 months, compared to 5.9 months for Group 2 and 5.6 months for Group 3 (F = 5.931, df = [2,203], p = .003); this may be due to earlier detection of their status through toxicology results at the time of birth. Almost half of the Group 1 infants (46%) were placed within the first month of life while less than a quarter of the Group 2 infants (21%) and Group 3 infants (22%) were placed during that time.

TABLE 1
Developmental Functioning and Health/Caregiving Needs (Mean)

	Mental Score 1	Mental Score 2	Motor Score1	Motor Score2	Number of Needs
Group1	81.16	87.85	85.36	86.97	2.03*
	(107)	(54)	(87)	(35)	(118)
Group 2	86.21	93.16	91.67	94.89	1.30*
	(33)	(19)	(27)	(9)	(33)
Group 3	82.51	88.64	84.14	86.86	1.85
	(35)	(14)	(29)	(7)	(39)
All Subjects	82.38	89.14	86.30	88.35	1.86
	(175)	(87)	(51)	(51)	(190)

Note: Within group means. Numbers in parentheses indicate the sample size for each mean. Asterisks indicate a significant difference ($p \leq .05$).

Cognitive and Motor Development

Scores of cognitive and motor development are presented in table 1. The first scores in cognitive and motor development were obtained when the infants were an average of 12.71 months of age, while the second scores were obtained when they were an average of 28.92 months of age. While there are no significant differences in functioning among the three groups (i.e., the infants with verified drug exposure did not score significantly better or worse than those with some suspicion or no suspicion of drug exposure), it is of interest that the total group of infants scored within the mildly delayed range (82.38) at the time of the first assessment, placing them all at an increased risk of later developmental delay. The second assessment of cognitive scores reflects an improvement in functioning (mean score 89.14); the change in scores, however, was not statistically significant.

Health and Caregiving Needs

In the area of health and caregiving needs, the three exposure groups differed significantly (F = 3.065, df = [2,187], p = .049) with the infants with verified drug exposure (Group 1) presenting with the most needs (X = 2.03) and with significantly more than the infants in Group 2 (X = 1.30; p = .014). The health and caregiving needs tabulated included such conditions as apnea, anemia, asthma, frequent ear infections, frequent colds, small size, vision or eye muscle problems, and sleep, feeding, and early behavior problems. While frequent colds and ear infections occurred in 21% to 28% of all groups, the infants with verified drug exposure had a higher incidence of asthma and small size, and a higher incidence of eating, sleeping, and early behavior problems. It should be noted that because children in Group 1 were exposed to as many as six different drugs, and because alcohol usage could not be ascertained and controlled for, these findings cannot unambiguously be interpreted as indicating drug effects without additional data and multivariate analysis. This finding, however, raises the question of a higher risk category for some infants possibly because of a greater level or degree of involvement in substance abuse by their mothers as signaled by the infants having drugs in their systems at the time of birth.

Visiting

The frequency of biological parents visits was rated on a four-point scale: 1 = no contact; 2 = rare contact; 3 = variable contact; and 4 = regular contact. Infants with verified exposure to drugs had markedly fewer parental visits than the other two groups of infants, with 75% of these infants falling into the "rare" contact or "no" contact classifications (figure 1). In contrast, 48% of infants with some suspicion of drug exposure and 36% of infants with no suspicion of drug exposure experienced "rare" or "no" contact from their biological parents. Infants with verified exposure to drugs had fewer of the "variable" or "regular" pattern of parental visits (25%), while infants with some suspicion of drug exposure had more of these visits (51%), and infants with no suspicion of drug exposure had most of these types of visits (64%).

FIGURE 1
Biological Parent Visiting

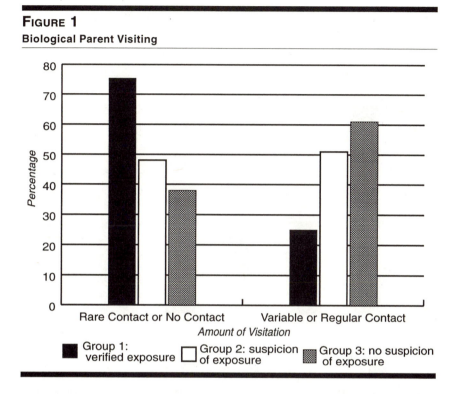

Length of Stay and Disposition

Length of stay did not differ among the groups and ranged from 21.1 months (Group 3 infants) to 28.4 months (Group 2 infants). Dispositions at the time cases were moved from the agency included: permanent placement (adoption or guardianship) with the agency's foster family; reunification with the biological parent(s); placement in the home of a relative; placement for permanence (adoption or guardianship) in a county family foster home; or other closure (e.g., to another out-of-home care system). Infants with verified exposure to drugs were more frequently placed with relatives (25% of cases) following foster placement, compared to 9% of infants with some suspicion of drug exposure, and 4% of infants with no suspicion of drug exposure (fig-

FIGURE 2

Placement at Disposition

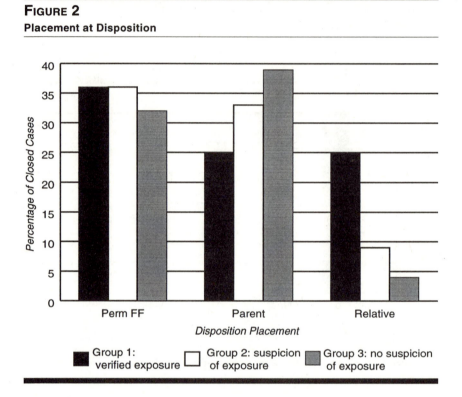

ure 2). Additionally, whereas 32% and 39% of infants with some suspicion and no suspicion of drug exposure respectively were placed with their biological parents following family foster care, only 20% of infants with verified drug exposure were placed with their biological parents. A similar proportion of infants in all three groups (36% of Group 1, 36% of Group 2, and 32% of Group 3) were permanently placed with the agency's foster parents.

Implications for Family Foster Care in the Next Century

The experience of a large, metropolitan foster family agency in caring for infants from 1990 through 1997 suggests that family foster care in the next century may be impacted in several ways.

This study found that infants placed in family foster care who were exposed to illegal drugs during gestation presented with a significantly greater number of health and caregiving needs than did other infants in family foster care. Because the infants with verified exposure to drugs during gestation constituted the largest group of infants in family foster care in this sample (61.7%), the impact of the needs presented by these infants is felt in all quarters. These needs place additional demands on the foster family, the foster care agency, and the medical/professional community, and require an enlightened response in terms of heightened awareness, training, access to services, continuity of care, follow-through, and application of appropriate treatments or interventions (as advocated by Blatt et al. [1997]). Because these same infants are more frequently placed in the homes of relatives following foster placement, these demands will then be placed upon these caregivers, indicating a need to include the relatives in training and support programs during the child's foster placement. The same emphasis on involvement and training applies to those biological parents who may resume care of their children. The health and special medical needs of these infants, which included a variety of conditions including anemia, asthma, small size, and feeding and sleeping problems, may be seen as normal by health care providers, while in reality, they are particular characteristics of this population, and thus may require added or aggressive treatment, monitoring, and follow-up care. With regard to caregiving problems (e.g., sleeping, eating, or early behavioral difficulties) these data suggest the need for a multidisciplinary approach that includes thorough assessment, and formulation and implementation of an individual, symptom-oriented intervention plan with training for all caregivers. Training and support should also be provided to all caregiving families prior to disposition to help them search out and obtain necessary services (e.g., special education programs, early intervention services) for their charges.

Other major findings of this study were that infants with verified drug exposure who were subsequently placed into family foster care (1) received fewer visits from their biological parents, and (2) were placed more often with relatives at the time of disposition (i.e., upon leaving the agency), compared to infants with some suspicion or no suspicion of drug exposure. These two factors—visiting and disposition—are undoubtedly interrelated and, along with the increase in health and caregiving needs, may be a secondary manifestation of the parents' degree of involvement in substance abuse. This degree of involvement in substance abuse may include issues of addiction and drug-seeking behaviors, health, transportation, lack of support, finances, lack of treatment options, and involvement in the legal system, which in turn could negatively impact parenting and which require intense, multisystem interventions. This finding also implies that the out-of-home care system must work to improve the frequency of visits by biological parents and to involve relatives in visiting early in the placement. The first job, increasing visiting for all family members, may require flexible visiting schedules (e.g., time, frequency, location). Requiring the biological parents and relatives of the child in family foster care to accompany their child to medical or diagnostic appointments and to intervention programs may also increase involvement and visits. Innovations in case planning, such as the Family Group Decision Making Model [Merkel-Holguin et al. 1997], that bring the nuclear and extended biological families into the program early in placement, have the potential for increasing the involvement and responsibility of all interested parties in providing for the long-term care of the child.

Although infants with verified drug exposure did not score significantly better or worse in cognitive functioning than other infants in family foster care, the group as a whole scored in a range that placed them at heightened risk of later significant developmental delay. The finding that the infants with verified drug exposure do not show additional cognitive deficits supports a similar result reported by Frank [1996]. The finding of low developmental functioning for all infants in care in this study, however, places a burden of obtaining intensive stimulation programs in the lap of the out-of-home care agency. An intensive program for these infants would include early, periodic, and multidisciplinary assessments using reliable and accepted measures of development, formulation of a multidisciplinary intervention plan, and the implementation of the plan utilizing services in the community and in the family foster home. To include both foster parents and caseworkers in a multidisciplinary team to identify and remediate developmental delays or lags would require specialized training.

As a group, the infants in this study made a gain in scores of cognitive functioning from the first to the second assessments. The improvement in scores may have continued to increase over time, indicating a need to continue measurement of development even past the time of closure or disposition, and to make efforts to identify the factors (e.g., qualities of foster parenting, type or frequency of interventions) that lead to change.

Although many infants were identified at the time of placement as having been exposed to illegal drugs during gestation, infants with other reasons for referral (e.g., neglect, physical abuse, domestic violence) may also have been exposed to illegal drugs during gestation. These infants should be identified as such and then considered as presenting with an increased risk of special health or caregiving needs, while their biological parents need to be identified as needing added help in visiting and regaining custody of their child.

In this study, cocaine was predominate as the drug affecting infants placed in family foster care, and thus, as a drug severely affecting their biological parents and extended families. Out-of-home care agencies need to support and encourage a societywide response to this problem in the form of research on the causes and treatment of cocaine abuse.

Final disposition often marks the end of the agency's involvement in a child's life. Funding, the legal system, and sometimes, an adversarial relationship with biological families make it difficult for foster family agencies to ensure continuity of caregiving, to follow progress of children, and to receive invaluable feedback about the effectiveness of family foster care. This process may result in the loss of a comprehensive view of the timing and the processes involved in change in the lives of these children and their families. Future case plans should emphasize the development of a collaborative relationship with biological parents and other relatives during the placement to set the stage for a voluntary and cooperative continuance of contact.

Limitations may exist in applying these findings to other agencies, children in family foster care, or geographical locations. Potential sources of error could exist in group assignment (e.g., unknown drug exposure of a Group 3 child) and other factors could account for or contribute to group differences (e.g., the use of alcohol or nicotine or the mother's nutritional status during gestation). Because this was not a cohort study, variables that could have changed during the years of this study (e.g., legislation governing timing and procedures for detaining children, determining placement, reunification, and disposition) may also have influenced its outcome.

Summary

In the next century, the task of family foster care in providing for the needs of infants exposed to drugs during gestation will be challenging in terms of providing quality care; monitoring progress; obtaining services; training staff and all caregivers; coordinating medical and community-based services; building relationships with biological parents and relatives; advocating for needs, services, and funding for the child and the biological family; and assessing effectiveness.◆

References

Azuma, S. D., & Chasnoff, I. J. (1993). Outcome of children prenatally exposed to cocaine and other drugs: A path analysis of three-year data. *Pediatrics, 92,* 396-402.

Blatt, S. D., Saletsky, R. D., Meguid, V., Church, C. C., O'Hara, M. T., Haller-Peck, S. M., & Anderson, J. M. (1997). A comprehensive, multidisciplinary approach to providing health care for children in out-of-home care. *Child Welfare, 76,* 331-348.

Chasnoff, I. J., Landress, H. J., & Barrett, M. E. (1990). The prevalence of illegal drug use or alcohol use during pregnancy and discrepancies in mandatory reporting in Pinellas County, Florida. *New England Journal of Medicine, 322,* 1202-1206.

Frank, E. J. (1996). Prenatally drug-exposed children in out-of-home care: Are we looking at the whole picture? *Child Welfare, 75,* 19-34.

Hurt, H., Brodsky, N. L., Betancourt, L., Braitman, L. E., Malmud, E., & Giannetta, J. (1995). Cocaine-exposed children: Follow-up through 30 months. *Developmental and Behavioral Pediatrics, 16,* 29-35.

Mattson, S. N., Riley, E. P., Gramling, L., Delis, D., & Jones, K. L. (1998). Neuropsychological comparison of alcohol-exposed children with or without physical features of Fetal Alcohol Syndrome. *Neuropsychology, 12,* 146-153.

Merkel-Holguin, L., Winterfield, A. P., Harper, C. J., Fluke, J. D., & Colburn, N. A. (1977). Innovations for children's services for the 21st century: Family group decision making and Patch. Englewood, CO: American Humane Association.

Phillips, R. B., Sharma, R., Premachandra, B. R., Vaughn, A. J., & Reyes-Lee, M. (1996). Intrauterine exposure to cocaine: Effect on neurobehavior of neonates. *Infant Behavior and Development, 19,* 71-81.

Vogel, G. (1997, October 3). Cocaine wreaks subtle damage on developing brains. *Science, 278,* 38-39.

Evaluation of a Training Program for Foster Parents of Infants with Prenatal Substance Effects

11

Caroline L. Burry

The lack of prepared and available foster parents for children with prenatal substance effects is of increasing concern to the child welfare field. The research study reported here evaluated a multimodal inservice training program designed to enhance the competency of foster parents caring for infants with prenatal substance effects, and to promote an intent to foster such infants. Findings suggest that future foster parent training efforts in this area should focus on knowledge and skill attainment.

Caroline L. Burry, Ph.D., is Assistant Professor, University of Maryland School of Social Work, Baltimore, MD.

One of the most critical current concerns in child welfare is meeting the needs of infants with prenatal substance effects.* The problem has three primary components. First, the increasing prevalence of these children in family foster care creates a need to increase the number of foster parents who will foster infants with prenatal substance effects. Second, those foster parents who are motivated to care for these infants may not have the skills, knowledge, confidence, or support they need to care for infants with prenatal substance effects. Third, infants with prenatal substance effects may require specialized care and foster parents need to be prepared to provide it. Effective foster parent training is needed to assure infants are fostered by knowledgeable, skilled foster parents and that the foster parents feel supported and effective in taking on their responsibilities.

Literature Review

A number of studies have documented the prevalence of mothers and neonates testing positive for the substances of drugs and alcohol, often in combination. An estimated 11% to 14.8% of infants in the U.S. test positive for illicit drugs at birth [Chasnoff et al. 1990; Kantrowitz 1990]. A prevalence rate of 11% means that approximately 375,000 drug-exposed babies are being born annually in the United States [Klebe 1989; "New Report" 1990]. Many researchers also believe that the incidence of substance abuse among pregnant women and the subsequent numbers of substance-affected births are increasing and will continue to increase in the future [Howard & Krospenske 1989; MacGregor et al. 1987; Weston et al. 1989].

The prevalence of substance-affected births is not the only factor supporting the need for research in this area. Infants with

---

* For the purposes of this study, *infants with prenatal substance effects* were defined as children from birth to age 2 who have had prenatal exposure to illicit drugs, alcohol, and/or higher than prescribed amounts of medications.

prenatal substance effects also have been found to have unique needs and characteristics. Although it is important not to stereotype these infants, a broad continuum of typical outcomes has been described in the literature. Some of the common problems for which infants with prenatal substance effects are at risk include developmental lags, prematurity, small size for gestational age, low Apgar scores, hypertonicity, hydrocephaly, apnea, stillbirth, heart and kidney malformations, and increased rates of Sudden Infant Death Syndrome [Blakeslee 1990; Chira 1990; Howard et al. 1989; Howard & Krospenske 1989; Kantrowitz 1990; Miller 1989; Tyler et al. 1997; Weston et al. 1989].

Typical characteristics that can make these babies challenging to parents are tremulousness, piercing cries, eating and sleeping disturbances, physical rigidity, irritability, and confused responses to stimulation. Caregivers for these infants not only need to know this array of characteristics, but they also need training in the special skills needed to deal with them [Chasnoff et al. 1985; Durfee 1990; Griffith 1989; Howard & Krospenske 1989; Schaffer 1990; Zuckerman 1993].

Adding support to the need for further research is the lack of available and appropriate foster homes, which has reached a crisis level. The complex needs of both substance-abusing mothers and their affected infants mean that out-of-home placement of the children is often necessary; an estimated 30% to 60% of infants with prenatal substance effects have had at least one out-of-home placement [Barth et al. 1994].

The increased need for family foster homes has not been matched by increases in family foster care resources. In fact, the lack of available family foster homes for these infants may be approaching a crisis level [Barth et al. 1994; Besharov 1994; Weston et al. 1989]. Barth noted that the greatest concern in child welfare is the expanding number of children affected by prenatal substance exposure [1991]. Overall, the numbers of foster families have fallen by a third nationwide since the mid-1980s [CWLA

1992]. This lack of family foster homes has led to a "category" of child that has come to be called the "boarder baby." Boarder babies are those infants medically cleared for release from hospitals who must stay in the hospital until foster placements are located; they are a great concern to child welfare professionals not only because of the high expenses of unnecessary hospital care but also because family care is considered to be much more appropriate for babies than is hospital care [Groze et al. 1994].

Even when foster parents are available for the placement of infants with prenatal substance effects, they have been found to have a higher burnout rate than do other foster parents. Foster parents of infants with prenatal substance effects have reported that one problem they face is a lack of support, typically described as a lack of a social support network with other foster parents who could provide services such as respite care. Other reported problems include a lack of knowledge and skills about fostering infants with prenatal substance effects [Edelstein et al. 1990]. Edelstein and colleagues further note that "the scarcity of foster homes in general, foster parent burnout, and the lack of supportive services for foster parents are all serious problems nationwide. The shortage of foster homes for perinatally exposed infants is even more critical, for these children strain the resources of even the most competent foster parents" [p. 318].

Hypotheses

The factors identified above that may influence the preparedness and availability of foster homes for these infants were the basis of the training tested in this research and the research hypotheses. The training included content designed to enhance foster parents' knowledge and skills about fostering infants with prenatal substance effects because of the previously described special needs of these infants. Efficacy content was included because of research findings about the significance of parental efficacy.

For instance, parental efficacy has been identified as an important variable in predicting outcomes for children with special needs, outcomes for depressed mothers, behavioral competence, and parental involvement in school [Cutrona & Troutman 1986; Hoover-Dempsey et al. 1992; Swick 1988; Rodrigue et al. 1990; Teti & Gelfand 1991; Teti et al. 1990].

The foster parent training tested in this research also included content designed to enhance the social support of the foster parent trainees, as the literature contains much evidence of the relationship of social support to effective parenting [Gowen et al. 1989; Seybold et al. 1991; Tucker & Johnson 1989] and to foster parenting [Barsh et al. 1983; Hazel et al. 1983; Henry et al. 1991; Simms 1983; Stone & Stone 1983; Urquhart 1989].

The research hypotheses were as follows:

1. The foster parents receiving an intervention of special training will have greater feelings of efficacy in caring for infants with prenatal substance effects after the training than before the training.

2. The foster parents receiving the training will be better able to demonstrate a set of specific skills for the caregiving of infants with prenatal substance effects after the training than before the training.

3. The foster parents receiving the training will be able to demonstrate more specific knowledge about infants with prenatal substance effects after the training than before the training.

4. The foster parents receiving the training will report greater feelings of social support in caring for infants with prenatal substance effects after the training than before the training.

5. The foster parents receiving the training will be more likely to intend to foster infants with prenatal substance effects after the training than before the training.

6. There is no relationship between demographic variables of the foster parents and changes in intent to foster, knowledge, skills, feelings of efficacy, or feelings of social support.

Methodology

Design

The research hypotheses in this study were tested by a pretest-posttest nonequivalent comparison group design. The treatment group received the specialized foster parent training and the comparison group was tested while attending televised foster parent training programs on other topics.

The independent variable in this research was an intervention of a specialized training program about foster parenting infants with prenatal substance effects. The dependent variables were feelings of efficacy about caring for infants with prenatal substance effects, demonstration of specific caregiving skills for these infants, attainment of specific knowledge about infants with prenatal substance effects, feelings of social support, and intent to foster infants with prenatal substance effects.

Assignment to Groups

True random assignment of subjects was impossible because of the voluntary nature of foster parent training; the samples of foster parents for both the treatment group and the comparison groups were therefore self-selected. Approximately 80 foster parents were allowed to register for various deliveries of the training. This oversampling was deliberate so that as many foster parents as possible would actually attend the training. The target number of foster parents for the treatment group established at the beginning of the research project was 30. Due to a variety of difficulties, this target was revised downward slightly to 28 during the study. The comparison group of 60 for this study was drawn from foster parents who were attending regionally televised foster parent training sessions.

Training Curriculum

The training curriculum was designed to be delivered in four weekly sessions of two-and-one-half hours per week for a total of ten hours. The training was designed so that the foster parents would have opportunities to achieve highly specific learning objectives. At the conclusion of the training, foster parent participants should have been able to describe whether and how they were prepared to deal with situations that might arise while fostering infants with prenatal substance effects; known some community and foster parent resources that might be useful to them in the future; been able to describe the care of a substance-affected infant in detail to another foster parent; and known their decisions about fostering infants with prenatal substance effects in the future.

Implementation Difficulties

The most challenging part of this research study was the difficulty of obtaining sufficient numbers of foster parents for the treatment group. Although originally scheduled to be concluded in six months, the data collection/foster parent training component of the research took almost two years. Recruitment efforts appeared to be effective and interest from prospective participants was high, with 80 registrants. Only 28 foster parents completed all of the training and instruments, however, although approximately twice that many attended at least one session of the training. Most of the foster parents who missed a session or sessions of the training indicated that they had had to miss due to the needs of the children they were fostering at the time.

Instrumentation

Six short, easy-to-administer instruments were used in this study. The first was the "Foster Parent Profile Questionnaire," developed by Dutes [1985], which gathered demographic information about foster parents. Foster parents' feelings of efficacy about foster parenting were measured using the Dutes "Foster Parent Parenting Efficacy Scale" (FPPES) [1985], which has an internal consistency reliability of .71. The Dutes version of the FPPES consisted of 10 statements about fostering. Respondents were asked to agree or disagree on a four-point Likert scale. Two additional items specifically about fostering infants with prenatal substance effects were added to this scale and analyzed separately.

Feelings of social support of foster parents were measured using an adapted version of the Parenting Social Support Scale [Telleen et al. 1989], which has a reported reliability of .71. The Parenting Social Support Scale asks parents about their needs for support in areas such as talking about their children and in receiving help with child care. Within each of these areas, three components of social support are examined: how much support the parents need in that area, who are their sources of support in that area, and how satisfactory was the support received in that area. The Parenting Social Support Scale was adapted and is here referred to as the Foster Parenting Social Support Scale (FPSSS).

Three additional instruments were designed by the researcher. The Skills Rating Sheet (SRS) was used to record foster parents' abilities to demonstrate specific caregiving skills for infants with prenatal substance effects. The skills, practiced during the training, included swaddling, vertical rocking, putting an infant down in a sidelying position, and carrying an infant in a flexed position. Foster parents in the training were videotaped demonstrating the four caregiving skills with a doll. Two raters independently viewed these videotapes and rated each participant.

The second instrument developed by the researcher was the Substance-Affected Infants Knowledge Inventory (SAIKI), a self-administered tool for measuring foster parents' knowledge about infants with prenatal substance effects. The SAIKI consisted of 10 true-false items. Two sample items from the SAIKI were, "Substance-affected infants need more stimulation than do other babies," and "Once a substance-affected baby goes through 'withdrawal,' he or she will be fine."

The final instrument developed by the researcher was the Intent to Foster (IF) instrument, used to collect data about the foster parents' intention to foster infants with prenatal substance effects.

Data Collection

The order in which the instruments were administered was counter-balanced. The trainers administered the instruments to the subjects in the treatment group as a pretest at the beginning of their first training sessions. The trainers administered all instruments except the FPPQ, the FPSSS, and the IF again during the final group training sessions as a posttest. Since the FPPQ was used to provide descriptive and demographic information about the foster parent subjects only, an additional administration was unnecessary. The FPSSS and the IF were mailed to the treatment group participants six weeks after training as a posttest.

The comparison group for this study completed the instruments while they were attending other foster parent training. The comparison group completed the Foster Parent Profile Questionnaires, the Foster Parent Parenting Efficacy Scale, the Foster Parent Social Support Scale, the Substance-Affected Infant Knowledge Inventories, and the Intent to Foster instruments only.

Data Analysis

Because of the paired sample design, the first four hypotheses generated for this study were tested using t-tests on the means in the treatment and comparison groups. The fifth hypothesis was tested using categorical data; therefore, a loglinear analysis was conducted. The final hypothesis was tested with correlations, since it had to do with comparisons of demographic data with results from the study instruments.

Descriptive Characteristics of the Treatment Group and Comparison Group

Information about the demographic characteristics of the 28 treatment group and 60 comparison group foster parents was obtained from the Foster Parent Profile Questionnaire. Similarities for the two groups included the age and education of foster parents, the types of special-needs children they had fostered, and the fact that they considered foster parenting to be a rewarding experience. Differences between the two groups included race, residential area, and number of children currently living in the home. It is speculated that the described demographic differences may be due to the small sample size. While the groups are nonequivalent, it appeared that they were similar enough that comparisons could be made between the two groups. The treatment group and comparison group were also compared with regard to their scores on several of the other instruments to learn whether any similarities in the two groups were due to chance. There were no statistically significant differences between the treatment and comparison groups on all study instruments, indicating the treatment group was likely to have been typical of foster parents who attend foster parent training.

Hypothesis Testing

An alpha level of $p = .01$ was used for all statistical tests. The hypotheses that were rejected, though reported at the $p = .01$ level, were also not accepted at the $p = .05$ level.

First Hypothesis. The first hypothesis, that the foster parents receiving an intervention of special training would have greater feelings of efficacy in caring for infants with prenatal substance effects, was tested using total scores on the Foster Parent Parenting Efficacy Scale (FPPES). Means were compared using t-tests. The first hypothesis was rejected because on both versions of the efficacy instrument, changes from pretest to posttest were not significant.

Second Hypothesis. The second hypothesis, that the foster parents receiving an intervention of special training would be able to demonstrate proficiency in a set of four specific skills for the caregiving of infants with prenatal substance effects, was tested using scores on the Skills Rating Sheet (SRS) as rated by two independent raters.

Before this hypothesis was tested, results from the two raters were compared through correlations on the four skills on the pretest and on the posttest. On the pretest skills, there were significant correlations between the two raters at the $p = .01$ level for all four skills. On the posttest, it was not possible to run a correlation on skills one and three because there was not enough variability in the raters' scores. On skill four on the posttest, there was a correlation of .6830 between the two raters, which was also significant at the $p = .01$ level. Given these results, interrater reliability was considered to be fairly high. Results for the raters were analyzed separately, however, because of the lack of variance described above.

Means on the pretests and posttests on the four specific skills were compared using t-tests. Results are presented in table 1.

The second hypothesis was accepted, based on the results of the analysis of the four skills in the SRS. Both raters found significant differences in skill attainment from pretest to posttest.

Third Hypothesis. The third hypothesis, that the foster parents receiving an intervention of special training would be able to demonstrate more specific knowledge about infants with prenatal substance effects, was tested using total scores on the Substance-Affected Infants Knowledge Inventory (SAIKI). The third hypothesis was accepted. The mean SAIKI score for the treatment group pretest was 6.26, with a standard deviation of 2.10. The mean score for the posttest was 8.37, with a standard deviation of 1.52. These means were compared and the t-value was 5.87, meaning that they were significantly different at the $p = .01$ level.

Fourth Hypothesis. The fourth hypothesis, that the foster parents receiving an intervention of special training would report greater feelings of social support in caring for infants with prenatal substance effects after the training than before the training, was tested using scores on the Foster Parent Social Support Scale (FPSSS). Results were analyzed and described on three subscales of the FPSSS: need for support subscale, sources of support

TABLE 1

Comparisons of Pretest and Posttest Skill Attainment

	Pretest		Posttest		
	M	*SD*	*M*	*SD*	*t-value*
Skill 1 (swaddling)					
Rater 1	2.11	.79	1.00	.00	7.45*
Rater 2	2.14	.89	1.25	.44	6.01*
Skill 2 (vertical rocking)					
Rater 1	2.79	.50	1.25	.52	12.75*
Rater 2	2.93	.38	1.36	.73	10.52*
Skill 3 (sidelying position)					
Rater 1	1.81	.74	1.07	.36	5.40*
Rater 2	1.86	.80	1.25	.52	4.36*
Skill 4 (flexed position)					
Rater 1	2.85	.37	1.68	.78	8.63*
Rater 2	2.82	.48	1.61	.88	6.72*

* Significant at the $p = .01$ level

subscale, and usefulness of support received subscale. Cross tabulations on these subscales were attempted, but due to the small sample size, there were too many empty cells to conduct an analysis. The fourth hypothesis was rejected. There was only a significant difference in the pretest and posttest means on the sources of support subscale. Those in the treatment group did not have a significant increase in social support in fostering infants with prenatal substances effects after attending the training.

Fifth Hypothesis. The fifth hypothesis, that the foster parents receiving an intervention of special training would be more likely to intend to foster infants with prenatal substance effects, was tested using loglinear analysis of scores on the Intent to Foster (IF) instrument. The calculated chi-square of the pretest and posttest results was 2.309 ($df = 1$). Since the critical value of chi-square at the $p = .01$ level of significance is 6.635, the fifth hypothesis was rejected.

Sixth Hypothesis. The sixth hypothesis, that there would be no relationship between demographic variables of the subjects and changes in the independent variables, was tested through a correlation using the Pearson's R test of the demographic data collected on the Foster Parent Profile Questionnaire (FPPQ) with the results of the other study instruments. The sixth hypothesis was accepted. Of all the correlations between the demographic variables of the subjects and the variables of intent to foster infants with prenatal substance effects, knowledge, skills, feelings of efficacy, or feelings of social support, only three correlations were significant. With the three minor exceptions, these results were as expected.

Summary and Discussion

Three of the six research hypotheses were accepted and three were rejected. It is speculated that an explanation for the lack of significant improvement in efficacy lies in the relatively high level of feelings of efficacy at pretest. From a programmatic point of view, these unexpected results are encouraging. That is, foster parents in both the treatment and control groups appeared to enter training with relatively high feelings of efficacy about fostering and about fostering substance-affected infants.

It appears that the specialized training did influence the attainment of four specific skills that have been found to be useful in caring for infants with prenatal substance effects, as well as the attainment of knowledge about these infants.

Those in the treatment group did not have a significant increase in social support in fostering infants with prenatal substances effects after the training. Therefore, as was considered with regard to efficacy, it may be that there was no strong need for improvement in social support in the foster parents studied. An alternate explanation is that treatment subjects did not increase significantly their feelings of social support because the training did not facilitate such an increase.

Although the results on the hypothesis regarding social support were not as expected, from a programmatic point of view they are encouraging. That is, foster parents in both the treatment and control groups in this study entered training with relatively high levels of social support. The review of the literature had indicated that lack of social support is related to foster parent burnout. That the foster parents in this study generally did not indicate a high need for support, had support available, and were mostly satisfied with the support they did have prior to entering training is promising in terms of the potential for lowered burnout among these foster parents.

There are several possible ways of considering the unanticipated results from testing the hypothesis on intent to foster infants with prenatal substance effects. It is possible that the training just did not influence intent to foster. Another way to consider these results, however, is to speculate that foster parents who chose to attend specialized training on fostering infants with prenatal substance effects had already made up their minds about fostering these infants and therefore their intentions were not influenced by the training. Finally, the possibility exists that some foster parents who attended the training decided as a result of the training not to foster infants with prenatal substance effects. If it is assumed that deciding not to foster infants with prenatal substance effects is an informed decision after attending specialized training, then this result may be considered positively.

Overall study results indicate that the specialized training on fostering infants with prenatal substance effects met at least two of the goals set for the training. That is, the training did appear to influence skill and knowledge attainment. Although the training goals for increasing efficacy, social support, and intent to foster were not achieved, it appears from the discussion above that programmatically, there were some positive findings in these three areas.

Implications

Although important implications may be drawn from this research, two limitations must be noted. First, even though it was similar in selected characteristics to the control group, the subject group was small, possibly limiting the study's generalizability. Second, it was not possible to control for the subjects' exposure to information on infants with prenatal substance exposure from sources other than the training (e.g., the media), and factors other than the training may have influenced outcomes.

This training may help meet some of the identified needs for prepared and available foster parents for infants with prenatal substance effects, a growing and underserved part of the child welfare population. Since current evidence suggests a continuing trend of expansion of family foster care for children with prenatal substance effects, this training could be a helpful response.

This study also suggests areas for future research. For example, the research reported here could be replicated with a larger group and the results compared. In view of the difficulties in retaining subjects through a four-session training format, it might be useful to consider a shorter training format, such as a two-session or even a long single-session format. Since knowledge and skills were most influenced by the training, additional content in those areas might be considered. As the knowledge base on infants with prenatal substance effects expands, future training will need to be updated to keep it state of the art. Future research might also extend and expand this training to later in the life span of children with prenatal substance effects.◆

References

Barsh, E. T., Moore, J. A., & Hamerlynck, L. A. (1983). The foster extended family: A support network for handicapped foster children. *Child Welfare, 62*, 349-359.

Barth, R. P. (1991). Adoption of drug-exposed children. *Children and Youth Services Review,* *13*, 323-342.

Barth, R. P., Courtney, M., Berrick, J. D., & Albert, V. (1994). *From child abuse to permanency planning: Child welfare services, pathways, and placements.* Hawthorne, NY: Aldine de Gruyter.

Besharov, D. J. (1994). *When drug addicts have children: Reorienting child welfare's response.* Washington, DC: Child Welfare League of America.

Blakeslee, S. (1990, May 19). Parents fight for a future for infants born to drugs. *The New York Times*, pp. A1, A9.

Chasnoff, I. J., Landress, H. J., & Barrett, M. E. (1990). The prevalence of illicit drug or alcohol use during pregnancy and discrepancies in mandatory reporting in Pinellas County, Florida. *New England Journal of Medicine, 322*, 1202-1206.

Chasnoff, I. J., Schnoll, S. H., Burns, W. J., & Burns, K. A. (1985). Cocaine use in pregnancy. *New England Journal of Medicine, 313*, 666-669.

Child Welfare League of America. (1992). *Boarder babies in selected hospitals in the United States: A survey.* Washington, DC: Author.

Chira, S. (1990, May 25). Crack babies turn 5, and schools brace. *The New York Times*, pp. A1, B5.

Cutrona, C. E., & Troutman, B. R. (1986). Social support, infant temperament, and parenting self-efficacy: A mediational model of postpartum depression. *Child Development, 57*, 1507-1518.

Durfee, M. (1990). *Drug/alcohol exposed neonates (Report).* Los Angeles: Child Abuse Prevention Program.

Dutes, J. C. (1985). *A comparative investigation of the effectiveness of two foster parent training programs* (unpublished doctoral dissertation, Michigan State University, 1985).

Edelstein, S., Krospenske, V., & Howard, J. (1990). Project T.E.A.M.S. *Social Work, 35*, 313-318.

Gowen, J. W., Johnson-Martin, N., Goldman, B. D., & Applebaum, M. (1989). Feelings of depression and parenting competence of mothers of handicapped and nonhandicapped infants: A longitudinal study. *American Journal on Mental Retardation, 94*, 259-271.

Griffith, D. R. (1989). Neurobehavioral effects of intrauterine cocaine exposure. *Ab Initio, 1(1),* 1-7.

Groze, V., Haines-Simeon, M., & Barth, R. (1994). Barriers in permanency planning for medically fragile children: Drug-affected children and HIV affected children. *Child and Adolescent Social Work Journal, 11,* 63-85.

Hazel, N., Schmedes, C., & Korshin, P. M. (1983). A case study in international cooperation. *British Journal of Social Work, 13,* 671-678.

Henry, D., Cossett, D., Auletta, T., & Egan, E. (1991). Needed services for foster parents of sexually abused children. *Child and Adolescent Social Work Journal, 8,* 127-140.

Hoover-Dempsey, K. V., Bassler, O. C., & Brissie, J. S. (1992). Explorations in parent-school relations. *Journal of Educational Research, 85,* 287-294.

Howard, J., Beckwith, L., Rodning, C., & Krospenske, V. (1989). The development of young children of substance-abusing parents: Insights from seven years of intervention and research. *Zero to Three, 9(5),* 8-12.

Howard, J., & Krospenske, V. (1989). A prevention/intervention model for chemically dependent parents and their offspring.

Kantrowitz, B. (1990). The crack children. *Newsweek, 66,* 62-63.

Klebe, E. (1989). *CBS report for Congress: "Crack" cocaine* (Report 89-428 EPW). Washington, DC: Congressional Research Service.

MacGregor, S. N., Keith, L. G., Chasnoff, I. J., Rosner, M. A., Chisum, G. M., Shaw, P., & Miller, G. (1989). Addicted infants and their mothers. *Zero to Three, 9(5),* 20-23.

New report on crack-cocaine and America's families. (1990, June). *Children's Voice,* 10.

Rodrigue, J. R., Morgan, S. B., & Geffken, G. (1990). Families of autistic children: Psychological functioning of mothers. *Journal of Clinical Child Psychology, 19,* 3711-379.

Schaffer, J. (1990). *Cocaine use during pregnancy: Its effects on infant development and implications for adoptive parents (Report).* Ithaca, NY: New York State Coalition for Children, Inc.

Seybold, J., Fritz, J., & MacPhee, D. (1991). Relation of social support to the self-perceptions of mothers with delayed children. *Journal of Community Psychology, 19,* 29-36.

Simms, M. D. (1983). The Foster Parenting Center: A multi-disciplinary resource for special needs preschoolers. *Infant Mental Health Journal, 4,* 116-125.

Stone, N. M., & Stone, S. F. (1983). The prediction of successful foster placement. *Social Casework, 64,* 11-17.

Swick, K. J. (1988). Parental efficacy and involvement: Influences on children. *Childhood Education, 65,* 37-42.

Telleen, S., Herzog, A., & Kilbane, T. L. (1989). Impact of a family support program on mothers' social support and parenting stress. *American Journal of Orthopsychiatry, 59* (3), 410-419.

Teti, D. M., & Gelfand, D. M. (1991). Behavioral competence among mothers of infants in the first year: The mediational role of maternal self-efficacy. *Child Development, 62,* 918-929.

Teti, D. M., Gelfand, D. M., & Pompa, J. (1990). Depressed mothers' behavioral competence with their infants: Demographic and psychosocial correlates. *Development and Psychopathology, 2,* 259-270.

Tucker, M. B., & Johnson, O. (1989). Competence promoting vs. competence inhibiting social support for mentally retarded mothers. *Human Organization, 48,* 95-107.

Tyler, R., Howard, J., Espinosa, M., & Doakes, S. S. (1997). Placement with substance-abusing mothers vs. placement with other relatives: Infant outcomes. *Child Abuse and Neglect, 21,* 337-348.

Urquhart, L. R. (1989). Separation and loss: Assessing the impacts on foster parent retention. *Child and Adolescent Social Work Journal, 6,* 193-209.

Weston, D. R., Ivins, B., Zuckerman, B., Jones, C., & Lopez, R. (1989). Drug-exposed babies: Research and clinical issues. *Zero to Three, 9*(5), 1-7.

Zuckerman, B. (1993). Developmental considerations for drug- and AIDS-affected infants. In R. Barth, J. Pietrzak, & M. Ramler (Eds.), *Families living with drugs and HIV.* New York: Guilford.